From Harvest to Home

SEASONAL ACTIVITIES, INSPIRED DECOR, AND COZY RECIPES FOR FALL

BY

Alicia Tenise Chew

PHOTOGRAPHS BY TOM MCGOVERN

Library of Congress Cataloging-in-Publication Data

Names: Chew, Alicia Tenise, author. | McGovern, Tom (Photographer)
  photographer.
Title: From harvest to home : seasonal activities, inspired decor, and cozy recipes for Fall /
  by Alicia Tenise Chew ; photographs by Tom McGovern.
Description: San Francisco, California : Chronicle Books LLC, [2022] |
Identifiers: LCCN 2021053526 | ISBN 9781797214344 (hardcover)
Subjects: LCSH: Entertaining. | Seasonal cooking. | House furnishings. | Handicraft. |
  Autumn--Miscellanea.
Classification: LCC TX731 .C5437 2022 | DDC 641.5/64--dc23/eng/20211231
LC record available at https://lccn.loc.gov/2021053526

Manufactured in China.

Design by Kelley Galbreath.
Food styling by Diana Jeffra.
Prop styling by Lauren Healy.
Typeset in Freight and Verlag.

Angostura (bitters) is a registered trademark of Angostura International Limited Company Canada;
Bluetooth is a registered trademark of Bluetooth Sig, Inc.; Elmer's is a registered trademark of Sanford,
L.P.; Fireball (whisky) is a registered trademark of Sazerac Brands, LLC; Frisbee is a registered trademark
of Wham-O Holding, Ltd.; Little Nell is a registered trademark of Aspen Skiing Company LLC; M&M's
is a registered trademark of Mars, Incorporated; Ping-Pong is a registered trademark of Indian Industries,
Inc.; Riesling is a registered trademark of Schmitt Söhne GmbH Weinkellerei; RumChata is a registered
trademark of Agave Loco LLC; Skittles is a registered trademark of Wm. Wrigley Jr. Company; Solo is
a registered trademark of Dart Container Corporation; Trader Joe's is a registered trademark of Trader
Joe's Company; X-Acto is a registered trademark of Sanford, L.P.; Zoom is a registered trademark of
Zoom Video Communications, Inc.

10 9 8 7 6 5 4 3 2 1

Chronicle books and gifts are available at special quantity discounts to corporations, professional
associations, literacy programs, and other organizations. For details and discount information, please
contact our premiums department at corporatesales@chroniclebooks.com or at 1-800-759-0190.

Chronicle Books LLC
680 Second Street
San Francisco, California 94107
www.chroniclebooks.com

Contents

November 109

Introduction

THERE'S SOMETHING SO REFRESHING ABOUT FALL. Despite being a grown woman, I always feel like I'm in the back-to-school mindset once September rolls around, and I have permission to start anew yet again. The nostalgia and coziness of the season always get me excited, year after year, without fail.

Goodbye beach vacations, barbecues, and sweltering heat. Hello to cooler temperatures, football season, apple picking, pumpkin patches, and, most important, gathering with friends and eating copious amounts of food. Honestly—any excuse to add more pumpkin, apples, and maple into my life is welcome, and one of the many reasons why I eagerly look forward to this wonderful time of year.

I, like many people, loved fall back when I was in high school. Don't get me wrong: Summer break was a blast, but I enjoyed getting back into my normal routine, performing at football games with my dance team, and making lifelong memories with friends. Growing up in Virginia, I found fall particularly beautiful. Every October, we'd watch as the Blue Ridge Mountains transformed from lush green into shades of gold, amber, and burgundy—a sight so stunning, it never failed to take my breath away.

My love for fall has only grown over the years, and as I get older, I appreciate it more and more. I personally believe it is the best season. Now that I'm an adult, the entertaining and travel possibilities during fall are unparalleled, and with all the activities, holidays, and events, there are so many opportunities for memory-making.

There was a brief period of time when I was reluctant to admit how much I loved fall. It was (and still is, by some) considered "basic" and predictable by my peers who were too cool for school. But guess what? This season is popular for a reason. I'm sure that you've made many memories over the years in the months of September, October, and November. That apple picking trip where you tried the best apple cider doughnut of your life. The leaf-peeping trip that made your jaw drop. The epic Halloween costume that you crafted all by yourself that you still show people photos of. The Friendsgiving where you met a new lifelong friend. Fall is a magical season: Don't let anyone make you feel less than for loving it and wanting to make the most of it.

Even though I never want fall to end, it seems to come and go in the blink of an eye. There's so much to do (and so much to eat!) that, at times, it can feel overwhelming. That's what inspired me to create this fall lifestyle guide. No need to research how to plan the perfect fall excursions or endlessly scroll Pinterest for the perfect seasonal recipes—I've rounded up all the best fall activities, DIYs, and elevated yet simple recipes in one spot so you can make the most of the season and create your own magic.

I am thrilled to help make your home and life a bit cozier during this glorious time of year. Now grab your pumpkin spice latte and your favorite sweater, sit back, and get inspired. Let's make this fall the best one yet.

September

APPLES, FOOTBALL, AND DECORATING THE HOUSE FOR THE NEW SEASON. These are a few of my favorite September things!

Fall might *technically* begin in late September each year in the northern hemisphere, but I like to start ushering in the season on September 1. By this point, I think we're all pretty eager for cooler temperatures and a change of pace. While most adults don't have school to look forward to, there's still something fresh about the month of September that makes you want to switch up your daily routine, try new things, and take advantage of everything the season has to offer.

The theme for the month of September is **transition**. Here, you'll learn how to ease into the new season with style and grace. For now, take your time—bid farewell to summer, adjust to the rhythms of the "school year," and savor every moment of the changing seasons. The fall equinox might not occur until later in the month, but by the time it rolls around, you'll feel fully prepared with these tips and ideas.

During this month, create your fall bucket list and start planning any fall travel, so you're able to make the most out of the season. It's also a perfect time to get organized: Figure out which activities you want to do, trips or events you want to prioritize, and recipes you want to try out with all those apples you'll pick at the orchard. Whatever you do, I encourage you to make this month your own, and maximize the opportunities where you can make memories.

ACTIVITY

The Ultimate Fall Bucket List

NOW THAT THE TEMPERATURES ARE STARTING TO COOL DOWN and the landscape is beginning to shift, it's the perfect time to plan how you want to take advantage of this magical season.

There are so many experiences and sights to take in during the fall. From apple picking and pumpkin patches, to leaf-peeping and baking with seasonal ingredients, fall is a very special time of year. (So much so that I've dedicated an entire book to it!)

First things first: Let's make an autumn game plan. I personally like to make my fall bucket list in the summer, during a heat wave—it's therapeutic for me. Once you have the list of activities down, get out your calendar and start making plans to knock off as much as possible on your bucket list. You might need to plan a trip spontaneously once you figure out when peak fall foliage is, but you can definitely plan a pumpkin patch date or a winery adventure ahead of time. →

Here Are a Few Ideas to Get You Started

- ☐ Decorate your home
- ☐ Book a leaf-peeping trip
- ☐ Visit a winery during harvest
- ☐ Go to a football game
- ☐ Host a tailgate party
- ☐ Visit a corn maze
- ☐ Go apple picking and get some treats at a local orchard
- ☐ Try a new apple recipe
- ☐ Carve or paint a pumpkin
- ☐ Roast pumpkin seeds or try a new pumpkin recipe

- ☐ Make your own pumpkin spice latte at home
- ☐ Craft your own Halloween costume
- ☐ Attend a haunted house
- ☐ Go on a hayride
- ☐ Rake your leaves (and jump in them afterward)
- ☐ Go on a hike
- ☐ Master a soup recipe
- ☐ Keep a gratitude journal and write down what you're grateful for daily
- ☐ Hire a professional photographer and take fall photos with your family (or friends!)

- ☐ Bake a pie
- ☐ Host a bonfire
- ☐ Craft your own spiced cider or mulled wine at home
- ☐ Have a movie night at home (scary movie marathon, anyone?)
- ☐ Host or attend a Friendsgiving or Thanksgiving celebration
- ☐ Burn a fall candle

Transition Your Wardrobe
FROM SUMMER TO FALL

FALL FASHION HAS AN EFFORTLESS QUALITY that makes it truly magical. The cozy sweaters, the stylish jackets, the showstopping boots— it's a much-needed, refreshing change of pace after spending your summer sweating in the same old clothes. I don't know about you, but I always feel inspired to try something new, refine my style, and step out of the house looking incredibly polished during the season!

As an adult, you might not get hooked up with a "back-to-school" wardrobe each year, but you can definitely add a few new pieces to your closet to celebrate the change in season. While fall trends come and go every year, there are a few timeless ways that you can transition your closet from summer to fall with ease. Let's face it: Fall weather can be pretty unpredictable depending on where you live, and it's always good to be prepared for any drastic change in temperature—whether it's warm or cold outside.

If you want to prep your closet for the new season, here are a few general tips and tricks to follow that will work annually.

- **FALL COLORS:** Start looking for pieces in darker tones or jewel tones. If it's still warm out, you can purchase hot-weather-friendly items in fall colors. Think of a breezy sundress in a burnt orange shade, or a pair of shorts in a deep plum color. That way, you look seasonally appropriate even if Mother Nature doesn't get the memo.

- **ANKLE BOOTS:** Swap out your sandals for ankle boots. You can easily wear ankle boots year-round: They look fantastic with dresses and also pair well with jeans and slacks. Plus, they work for any occasion: work, school, church, you name it!

- **FAUX LEATHER:** Faux leather will always be in style during the fall. Shorts, skirts, and jackets in this fabric are a solid bet.

- **SWAP OUT YOUR HANDBAG:** Put your straw and wicker bags in storage, and opt for a sleek leather or faux-leather handbag option.

- **LAYERS, LAYERS, LAYERS:** Throw on a jacket, layer a T-shirt or turtleneck underneath one of your favorite summer dresses, or pair a cozy knit sweater with a dress, skirt, or pair of slacks to bring your favorite summer pieces into the new season.

- **TIGHTS OR LEGGINGS:** Getting chilly out? Add a pair of tights or leggings for warmth. Both of these items are classics that will never go out of style.

- **WHEN IN DOUBT, ADD SOME PLAID:** This print is in style season after season, and is very versatile. Instantly pull together a look with a plaid shirt, skirt, slacks, or dress.

The Timeless Summer-to-Fall Transition Shopping List

- ☐ Denim jacket
- ☐ Faux-leather jacket
- ☐ Button-down shirt
- ☐ Updated pair of jeans
- ☐ Dresses you can wear in the heat of summer and also later in the season with layers
- ☐ Ankle boots
- ☐ Items in classic fall colors: Rust, oxblood, and marigold never seem to go out of style!
- ☐ Lightweight sweaters
- ☐ Anything plaid—tops, bottoms, or dresses

UPDATE YOUR
Home Decor for Fall

IF YOU'RE ANYTHING LIKE ME, you'll take any excuse to redecorate your home. I personally think that a new season calls for a freshening up of your space—especially when you plan to gather friends and family in your home for entertaining purposes.

I know what you're thinking: You might not have an endless amount of money to completely renovate your home just for one season. Luckily, you don't have to spend a ton of money to update your space for fall. By simply adding some budget-friendly seasonal accents, you can completely transform your space and make it feel incredibly cozy and inviting.

The smallest changes will make the biggest difference in your home when transitioning to fall. Here are a few ways that you can update your home decor for the change in season!

Swap Out Your Pillows and Throws

One budget-friendly way to update your home decor is to change out your pillows and throws. Pillows can add up, so try to find a color or a seasonal neutral pillow that mixes in with the existing pillows you have, such as a plaid or a knit cream pillow, rather than buying a completely new set for the season.

Also, you can never have too many throw blankets. They're great for the cooler temps and for hosting—guests tend to appreciate having options. (I'm not going to lie: I appreciate a good variety of throw blankets.) Play around with different seasonal colors and textures to transform your living room or bedroom into a fall wonderland.

Decorate Whimsically with Pumpkins

Who doesn't love some good pumpkin decor? Decorate with a mix of real and faux pumpkins. Use larger pumpkins outdoors for your stoop, and place mini pumpkins on the kitchen table, coffee table, bookcases, mantel, and anywhere else you have space! Try amassing a collection of Cinderella pumpkins and small gold votive candles down the center of your dining table for a kind of table runner.

Add Some Greenery

Bring the outside in and add some seasonal plants to your decor this fall. Eucalyptus leaves are a go-to. They look fantastic in garlands or floral arrangements, or on their own in a vase. Other natural elements you can use in your fall decor include mums, asters, pussy willow, pampas grass, and dusty miller.

Introduce Seasonal Colored Accents

Want to make your home feel even cozier? Add some warmer-toned decorative accents! Look for small decorative items, such as a table runner, napkin rings, coasters, or place mats, in the shades of burnt orange, charcoal, marigold, berry, beige, dusty rose, aubergine, deep green, persimmon, or chocolate to transform your space.

Deck Out Your Mantel

We typically decorate our mantel each year for the holidays—why not do the same in the fall? Some things you can add to your mantel in the fall: small and Cinderella pumpkins (and other gourds!), wooden accents, eucalyptus garlands, colorful foliage, Halloween displays, elegant candlesticks, and more. Feel free to mix textures here and make the mantel your own!

Add Spooky Elements in October

If you celebrate Halloween, go all out with the spooky touches this season. I love adding a lot of black accents like votive candles and throw blankets, black floral arrangements (you can purchase black faux florals or simply use very dark red or purple calla lilies, hellebore, or dahlias), spiderwebs, skulls, and other spooky touches to get in the spirit.

Try All the Fall Decor DIYs

Another way to not break the bank while redecorating for fall? Attempt some fall decor DIYs instead of buying new items in a store. On page 26, you can learn how to create your own fall wreath, page 73 shows you how to craft gold leaf pumpkins, and on page 74, you can make your own spooky decor ideas for Halloween.

DECOR & DIY

Decorate Your Stoop

FOR FALL

FALL IS A GREAT TIME TO BE OUTSIDE. With the milder temperatures, all the cozy layers you're able to wear, and the endless number of seasonal activities available, it's likely that you and your neighbors won't want to stay indoors too much during this time of year.

If you're spending more time outdoors, and potentially entertaining guests as well, September is the perfect time to update your stoop for the season. From wreaths to lanterns to gourds, there are so many ways to make your home's exterior look seasonal and fun.

Looking to spruce up your stoop for the season? Here are a few eye-catching ways you can update your home's exterior for fall!

Choose a Theme

When you're planning out your fall decor, choose a theme or a color palette to loosely follow so that your stoop, and your home, look cohesive and well thought out. Some theme options are harvest; spooky Halloween or cute Halloween; or white and gold.

Pick a Favorite Doormat (and Layer It!)

Whether you live in an apartment or a spacious home, the first thing you can do to update your outdoor fall decor is to swap out your doormat.

Also: Consider layering your doormat for a bit more personality. I'm a big fan of layering a larger black-and-white buffalo check doormat underneath a fall-themed doormat. The neutral tones of the black-and-white doormat pair perfectly with most any autumnal doormat.

Add a Fall Wreath

A fall wreath is apartment/condo friendly, and a great way to add a pop of fall color to your outdoor space and entryway. It's easy to find

fall wreaths at home decor shops at various price points; however, it is pretty simple to make a wreath of your own as well. Head to page 25 to see how to craft your own festive wreath!

Snag a Couple of Lanterns

Lanterns are a fun decor piece that you can leave on your porch or doorstep year-round, but for whatever reason, they work especially well for fall. Get funky with gold, go for a natural look with rattan lanterns, or opt for a sleek set of black lanterns. The possibilities abound!

Bring in Plants

Mums are the quintessential fall plant, and they look perfect on a stoop. Mums come in a variety of colors: everything from white to yellow, pink, lavender, red, and bronze. I love using mums as a pop of color on my doorstep. They also come in a range of sizes—if you have a smaller stoop, a medium-size mum plant would work perfectly. The larger your porch, the larger the mums should be.

Don't Forget the Gourds

Last but certainly not least: Add your favorite pumpkins to your stoop. The limit really doesn't exist here—you can use as many or as few pumpkins as you'd like.

If you're opting for multiple pumpkins, get a variety of different colors, sizes, and shapes of pumpkins. Your local pumpkin patch and/or grocery store should have "fantasy" pumpkins available—these specialty gourds come in beautiful, muted shades of white, green, yellow, and orange.

Using the Tips Above, Here Are Two Front Stoop Decor Ideas

- **PURPLE, GREEN, AND CREAM PALETTE:** If you're not feeling the classic orange and black color scheme this year, try a purple, green, and white look. Place an odd number of aluminum planters filled with purple and white mums on either side of your entryway (things look better in odd numbers!). Look for green and purple kale or cabbage plants at the market; these leafy greens look absolutely stunning in planters on their own. Intermingle some green and white

pumpkins, squash, and gourds in various sizes. Stack them, pile them in shallow bowls or planters, or artfully place them around the base of the planters you're using. Add a festive doormat and a green eucalyptus wreath. It's seasonal, but with a twist.

- **FARMHOUSE CHIC:** For a chic farmhouse look, go for neutral materials and colors like cream, burlap, and raw wood. Place a few white pumpkins around your stoop—you could also incorporate a few pale-colored pumpkins, if you like, but nothing too bright. Look for some rustic signage and weathered whitewashed lanterns. Low wood planters with white mums or tall aluminum planters with pampas grass will go nicely with this aesthetic. If you have space, add a rocking chair or a small bench with weather-resistant pillows and a blanket, again in a neutral color. Keeping an understated color scheme will create a cozy, rustic vibe.

DIY Fall Wreath

WHETHER YOU LIVE IN AN APARTMENT or are settled into a single-family home, one thing is for sure: Your door will look very festive with a wreath on it. Now, it's pretty easy to shop for a fall wreath in stores and online. However, where's the fun in getting a premade wreath when you can make one yourself?

This fall, give a DIY wreath project a try. They're fairly easy to construct, and by making your own, you can customize it exactly to your liking. And who wouldn't want a custom fall wreath that matches their decor perfectly? The best part about this is that you don't have to stick to a traditional fall color palette—you have the freedom to swap out florals, types of greenery, and ribbon, incorporating any hues and textures you'd like.

This particular how-to creates a style that is pretty and autumnal. I like to use a 12 in [30.5 cm] wreath for indoor decor, but you can go big with an outdoor wreath—anywhere from 22 to 36 in [56 to 91 cm], depending on the width of your door.

This is a great project to do with friends or the kiddos on the weekend—imagine seeing everyone else's unique designs! Just get an assortment of greenery, faux flowers, ribbons, and other accessories. Plus, it will make you feel like a professional floral designer.

MATERIALS AND TOOLS

Wire wreath frame (12 in [30.5 cm] frame for an indoor wreath)

Black spray paint (optional)

Floral shears

3 or 4 eucalyptus branches (you can use a mix of baby blue eucalyptus and seeded eucalyptus)

10 to 20 small cedar branches

Wire cutters

Floral wire

Hot glue gun

3 to 5 faux white mini pumpkins

4 to 6 bunches of real or faux fall flowers, such as ranuculus, garden roses, dahlias, or zinnias (faux flowers will last much longer)

Berries, pinecones, or other natural elements (optional)

continued

DECOR & DIY

1 If desired, spray-paint the wire wreath frame with black paint before starting. Two or three coats of spray paint should do the trick. Be sure to spray-paint outdoors and wait at least 30 minutes in between coats. Wait a day for the spray paint to fully dry before continuing on to step 2.

2 Using floral shears, cut the eucalyptus and cedar branches into smaller pieces that are roughly the same length, about 6 to 8 in [15 to 20 cm] each. Using wire cutters, cut your floral wire into pieces 4 to 5 in [10 to 12 cm] in length.

3 Working your way around the wire wreath frame, use the pieces of floral wire to attach the greenery, alternating between the cedar branches and the eucalyptus. About 1 in [2.5 cm] up from the bottom of a piece of greenery, bind the stem to the frame by wrapping a piece of wire around it a few times to secure. Try to overlap the stems so the wire on one piece of greenery is covered by another piece; by the time you finish, you shouldn't be able to see any wire. Continue until you have a nice base of greenery all the way around.

4 Using the hot glue gun, attach the faux mini white pumpkins to the wreath as desired.

5 Fill in any empty spots with flowers. If using faux flowers, cut off the stems and attach the flowers to the wreath using the hot glue gun. If using real flowers, cut the stems so they are about 3 in [8 cm] in length. Nestle the flowers into the greenery and use floral wire to secure the stem to the wire frame. If you have berries, pinecones, or other natural elements, feel free to tuck those in too.

6 Let dry overnight, and voilà! You're ready to hang your fall wreath.

VARIATIONS

- Instead of flowers, add a ribbon. Use a wide, wired ribbon—I like a black-and-white buffalo check or a metallic ribbon—and weave it through the greenery. Tie a big bow on the bottom in the center or slightly off to the side.

- Instead of using greenery like eucalyptus or cedar branches, collect as many colorful fallen leaves as you can find around your neighborhood (or use magnolia leaves, which are also beautiful!). Dry and flatten them a bit by leaving them spread out between two layers of newspaper overnight with a few books placed on top. When ready to assemble, use wire and/or a hot glue gun to affix the leaves to a wire wreath frame. Go around the circle multiple times to create lots of layers of leaves, and position them at slightly different angles. The more layers you add, the more bountiful it will look, plus you'll get lots of pretty overlapping colors. You could tuck in a few sprigs of red berries, or spray the final wreath with some gold glitter spray paint, if you'd like.

DECOR & DIY

WATCH IT!

The Best Football Movies and TV Series

THERE'S SOMETHING ABOUT AMERICAN FOOTBALL that makes it such a captivating sport. From cheering on your high school team during homecoming to tailgating NFL games as an adult, football is pretty much synonymous with fall.

It turns out that football also makes for some of the best storylines in film. Between hard-hitting dramas and lighthearted comedies, there are some incredible TV shows and movies about the beloved sport.

If you're pumped for football season, or if your favorite sport just isn't being aired one night, why not binge-watch some of these classic football movies and TV shows? →

Top Ten Classic Football TV Shows and Movies

- **ALL AMERICAN (2018-)**–This teen drama is about a star football player who is recruited from his humble South Los Angeles home to play at a school in Beverly Hills. This show tackles the subjects of class and race in an ambitious, spectacular way.

- **BALLERS (2015-2019)**–In this show, a retired pro football player tries to reinvent himself as a financial manager to some of the best NFL players—with comedic results.

- **FRIDAY NIGHT LIGHTS (2006-2011)**– Arguably, *Friday Night Lights* is the best football TV show of all time. This critically acclaimed series is based in Texas and follows one of the most winningest football teams in the country— and their struggles on and off the field.

- **ANY GIVEN SUNDAY (1999)**–This powerful sports drama gives you a glimpse at the ups and downs of the football world. Plus, Al Pacino's speech in this movie is an iconic moment.

- **DRAFT DAY (2014)**–A general manager of an NFL team faces a big dilemma: either rebuild his team or abandon them for another team and a number-one draft pick. Does he make the right decision?

- **JERRY MAGUIRE (1996)**–A rom-com meets sports drama? Sign me up. This classic sports flick stars Tom Cruise as Jerry Maguire, who is forced to start his own sports management firm after a blunder at his former employer.

- **THE LONGEST YARD (1974)**–A movie so good that Adam Sandler decided to do a remake. In this film, an ex-football player and current prison inmate is forced to organize a team of fellow convicts to play against prison guards.

- **REMEMBER THE TITANS (2000)**–At a Virginia high school in the 1970s, football is a time-honored tradition. When this school is forced to integrate with a local all-Black school, the community must come together and address major civil rights issues.

- **THE REPLACEMENTS (2000)**–In need of some comedic relief? This film follows the owner of the Washington Sentinels as he scrambles to find players to replace the ones that went on strike right before the playoffs.

- **RUDY (1993)**–This critically acclaimed movie follows Rudy, an aspiring University of Notre Dame football player, as he struggles to beat the odds, gain admission to the prestigious school, and qualify for their football team.

The Ultimate Tailgate Checklist

EVERY SEPTEMBER, I REJOICE because of the return of football. Friday through Sunday, I have an excuse to root for my favorite teams, gather with friends to watch the game, and—my favorite part—eat all the delicious game-day snacks.

Tailgating is one of my favorite fall traditions. Admittedly, I didn't go to a college with a football team, but I had several friends who were very passionate about their alma mater teams and brought me to games after I graduated. My life was changed for the better after that first tailgate. The energy, the food, the spirit—I was there for it all. If any of my friends ever needed to adopt a college football fan for a day, I was their girl.

The idea of hosting your own tailgate party can be a bit daunting to a novice host. Not only do you need to bring a ton of equipment to cook the food properly, but you're also in charge of the entertainment, power, and making sure your guests are comfortable, no matter what the weather is. However, with the right prep, you can host a tailgate party like a pro.

Whether you're tailgating at a stadium or throwing an epic football party at your own home, here is the ultimate tailgate checklist that will ensure you have the best time cheering on your team. ➡

Everything You Need for the Ultimate Tailgate

THE ESSENTIALS

- ☐ Team apparel
- ☐ Team flag, pole, and holder
- ☐ Folding table(s)
- ☐ Folding chairs
- ☐ Tablecloth
- ☐ Cooler(s)
- ☐ Ice
- ☐ Pop-up canopy or umbrellas
- ☐ Generator and gas
- ☐ Extension cords
- ☐ Garbage bags

GRILLING

- ☐ Grill
- ☐ Grilling tools
- ☐ Propane or charcoal, depending on grill
- ☐ Lighter and lighter fluid
- ☐ Mesh food net
- ☐ Disposable plates
- ☐ Disposable cups
- ☐ Disposable utensils
- ☐ Napkins
- ☐ Oven mitts

BEVERAGES

- ☐ Still and sparkling water
- ☐ Soda
- ☐ Beer
- ☐ Wine
- ☐ Liquor
- ☐ Drink mixers

UTENSILS

- ☐ Spatula
- ☐ Tongs
- ☐ Serving spoons
- ☐ Can opener
- ☐ Bottle opener
- ☐ Corkscrew
- ☐ Aluminum foil
- ☐ Cooking pots and saucepans
- ☐ Skewers
- ☐ Serving plates and bowls
- ☐ Freezer bags

CONDIMENTS

- ☐ Ketchup
- ☐ Mustard
- ☐ Mayonnaise
- ☐ BBQ sauce
- ☐ Relish
- ☐ Pickles
- ☐ Chopped onions
- ☐ Salsa and other dips
- ☐ Salt and pepper
- ☐ Other seasonings of your choice (Old Bay is a solid bet!)

ENTERTAINMENT AND GAMES

- ☐ Wireless Bluetooth speaker
- ☐ TV (to watch the game wherever you're parked)
- ☐ Frisbee
- ☐ Playing cards
- ☐ Cornhole/beanbag toss
- ☐ Bocce lawn game
- ☐ Table tennis set

MISCELLANEOUS ITEMS

- ☐ Game-day tickets
- ☐ Sunscreen
- ☐ Blankets
- ☐ Ponchos
- ☐ Phone chargers
- ☐ Flashlights
- ☐ Sunglasses
- ☐ Bungee cords
- ☐ First aid kit
- ☐ Duct tape
- ☐ Paper towels
- ☐ Wet wipes
- ☐ Hand sanitizer
- ☐ And don't forget the food! Burgers, hot dogs, buns, ribs, potato salad—whatever it is you plan to cook!

Sweet Potato Nachos

SERVES 4 TO 6 | **PREP TIME** 10 MINUTES | **TOTAL TIME** 40 MINUTES

NACHOS ARE A CLASSIC SNACK ON GAME DAY. How could you not love them? They're delicious, a total crowd-pleaser.

These are a fun twist on traditional nachos. Instead of tortilla chips, we're using sweet potatoes as chips. It's a slightly—emphasis on the slightly—healthier option that's still incredibly tasty.

Use a mandoline to slice the sweet potatoes into equal circles, but if you don't have one, a knife will work just fine.

FOOD

INGREDIENTS

½ tsp kosher salt
½ tsp cumin
½ tsp garlic powder
½ tsp chili powder
2 large sweet potatoes
2 Tbsp coconut oil, melted
½ cup [80 g] canned black beans, drained
½ cup [80 g] canned corn, drained
1 cup [80 g] shredded Monterey Jack cheese
1 avocado, peeled, pitted, and cut into ¼ in [6 mm] slices
¼ cup [35 g] diced red onion
1 green onion, cut into ¼ in [6 mm] slices
¼ cup [10 g] chopped cilantro
Salsa (optional)
Sour cream (optional)

1 Preheat the oven to 400°F [200°C] with a rack positioned in the center of the oven.

2 In a small bowl, mix together the salt, cumin, garlic powder, and chili powder.

3 Cut the sweet potatoes crosswise into ¼ in [6 mm] rounds. Place in a large bowl and toss with the coconut oil.

4 Spread the sweet potatoes onto a rimmed baking sheet in one layer and season with half of the salt mixture.

5 Roast the potatoes for 15 minutes. Flip over all the pieces, season with the remaining salt mixture, and roast for an additional 15 minutes or until the potatoes are crisp.

6   Top the potatoes with the black beans, corn, and cheese. Bake for 5 minutes or until the cheese has melted.

7   Top with the avocado, red onion, green onion, and cilantro.

8   Serve hot, with salsa and sour cream, if you'd like.

TAILGATE BITES

Root Vegetable Crackers with Whipped Goat Cheese Topping

SERVES 6 | **PREP TIME** 15 MINUTES | **TOTAL TIME** 45 MINUTES

FOOD

I'LL NEVER FORGET THE TIME my friend brought me to a football game at the University of Texas at Austin. Having never experienced a tailgate before, let alone a Texan tailgate, I felt like a fish out of water. There were blocks and blocks of booths with food and drinks, and a good chunk of the city shut down to celebrate the team. Between the delicious food and the passionate fans, it was an unforgettable experience. After that first tailgate, I became hooked, and volunteered to root for any of my friends' favorite teams if they brought me along on game day!

Twenty-year-old Alicia would have been content with pizza and wings on game day—and there's absolutely nothing wrong with those dishes. They're classics! However, if you're aiming to elevate your game-day experience, these root vegetable crackers will dazzle your guests at your next tailgate party.

INGREDIENTS

1 small sweet potato
1 large parsnip
1 small rutabaga
1 medium turnip
2 Tbsp coconut oil, melted
1 tsp kosher salt
½ tsp freshly ground black pepper
4 oz [115 g] goat cheese
1 Tbsp heavy cream
1 cup [140 g] dried cranberries
¼ cup [5 g] fresh rosemary, chopped
2 Tbsp honey, for drizzling

1 Preheat the oven to 400°F [200°C] with a rack positioned in the center of the oven.

2 Cut the sweet potato, parsnip, rutabaga, and turnip into round slices ¼ in [6 mm] thick. In a large bowl, toss the vegetables with the melted coconut oil.

3 Spread the vegetable slices out on a rimmed baking sheet in a single layer. (The closer they are, the more likely they are to steam; we want these to be crispy, so the more space between slices the better.) Season with the salt and pepper.

4 Bake the vegetables in the oven for 15 minutes. Flip each piece over and bake for an additional 15 minutes or until the vegetables are crisp. Let cool on the pan.

5 Meanwhile, in a small bowl, whisk together the goat cheese and heavy cream until smooth.

6 Top each root vegetable "cracker" with the whipped goat cheese mixture and a sprinkle each of the dried cranberries and rosemary, and transfer them to a platter or board. Drizzle with the honey and serve.

Harvest Winery Trip

(AND THE BEST WINES FOR FALL)

FALL IN THE NORTHERN HEMISPHERE is a pretty magical season for wine lovers. From August through October, vineyards are lush and brimming with fruit, and grapes reach their peak ripeness, which means one thing: harvest season. During the harvest, workers rush to pick their grapes, and often, wine regions across the United States will plan events and festivals to celebrate the end of the growing season. All in all, it's a glorious time to visit a winery.

Visiting wineries in the fall is great for several reasons. For starters, you have the chance to see the flush vines in all their glory. It is one of the most beautiful times of the year to visit. If you book a vineyard tour, there's a chance you'll be walked through the vines, and you might get a glimpse of the fruit at its peak. Plus, the temperatures tend to cool off, and it's comfortable to sit outside and enjoy the wine and the views.

If you are planning a winery trip in the fall, here's my best advice: Hire a driver for the day and ask them for the best routes, or pick a friend to be the designated driver and map out your trip in advance, especially if you're not familiar with the area you're going wine tasting in. Wineries tend to be pretty spread out, and you don't want to lose time sitting in the car just because a poor route was planned. Ask a local to get both the best route and an insider perspective. Who knows? You might come across an under-the-radar boutique winery that you never would have found if not for their recommendation!

The Best Wines for Fall

White Wines: White wine isn't just for warmer weather. For fall, opt for more full-bodied white wines. Full-bodied whites are heavier wines with more complex flavors and bold tasting notes. These wines are generally creamy and nutty, and have more aromatic character than light- or medium-bodied white wines. I find they pair well with classic fall dishes, like risotto, butternut squash, roasted veggies, potatoes, and pumpkin pie. The following are a few full-bodied white wines to try for fall.

- **CHENIN BLANC:** Chenin Blanc is a French varietal that can range from dry to sweet, and pairs well with both meat and side dishes without overpowering them. This wine typically has notes of apple, honey, and nutmeg.

- **WHITE RHÔNE (MARSANNE-ROUSSANNE):** This wine is a great alternative to try this fall if you're a fan of Chardonnay. It is slightly spicy, refreshing, and has notes of apricot and orange zest. Pair this with savory, buttery dishes.

- **SÉMILLON:** Sémillon is a full-bodied wine with notes of lemon, papaya, and green apple, and has medium acidity. Pair this wine with your fall dishes that have cinnamon, saffron, and/or star anise spices.

Red Wines: Fall is not only a great time to transition your wardrobe but also a fantastic time to switch up your wine rack. While I'm a firm believer in drinking whatever type of wine you like at any time of the year, the pairing of a red wine and a crisp autumn day screams perfection. Here are a few red varietals to try for fall.

- **CABERNET FRANC:** Fun fact: The Cabernet Franc and Sauvignon Blanc grapes crossed to form the Cabernet Sauvignon grape back in the 1600s. Cabernet Franc is known for its green pepper tasting notes and pairs well with earthy dishes, wild game, and lamb.

- **MALBEC:** Malbec is a French grape that thrives in Argentina. It's a full-bodied, peppery, spicy wine that is a perfect pairing for steak and other red meats.

- **ZINFANDEL:** Another full-bodied red to try in the fall is a Zinfandel. I prefer the richer Zinfandels from California for the season: They typically have sweet smoke and jammy tasting notes, and they taste heavenly with pumpkin and turkey dishes.

Apple Picking

WHAT BETTER WAY TO KICK OFF FALL than participating in the beloved tradition of apple picking?

There's a natural magic in enjoying a local orchard with friends, family, or loved ones; picking apples in the crisp, fall air; and enjoying delicious apple snacks at a picnic table afterward.

Apple picking is one of my favorite ways to kick off the fall season, and if you haven't been yet, here are a few ways to plan the perfect apple picking adventure.

Best Time of Year to Go Apple Picking

Did you know that apple picking is available in almost all fifty US states and Canada as well? That means there's a very high likelihood that apple picking is available near your home!

Generally, you'll want to plan your apple picking trip sometime between September and early October. Apple ripening season will vary from year to year, and this is mainly subject to the weather during the growing season. Depending on where you live, though, September and October are likely good bets—just check with your local apple farm before planning your visit.

What to Wear While Apple Picking

Let's be real: Apple picking in an orchard is a great photo op. However, you'll want to don an outfit that's both practical and stylish.

Orchards are working farms—which means they're full of dirt, mud, and possibly some animal droppings. Plus, there's a chance that you might need to partake in a short hike just to get to the orchard. Skip the heels and pick a comfy pair of sneakers that you don't mind getting dirty or a pair of rain boots that you can easily rinse off.

Leave your dresses at home and opt for a comfy pair of jeans and a flannel on top of a T-shirt. A flannel will keep you warm;

however, layer a T-shirt underneath just in case you get hot. Don't forget to bring a hat for sun protection.

Another tip for apple picking ensembles? I like to be hands-free if I can, so if you carry a purse, choose a small crossbody and only put the essentials in there!

How to Pick Apples Properly

Before heading off on your apple picking adventure, it's a good idea to ask the employees at the orchard which trees are ripe for picking before your visit.

How can you tell when an apple is ripe? If you can easily remove the stem of an apple from a branch, that means it is ready to pick.

Avoid bruised apples—these apples will rot faster and taint other apples in your bag. Be sure to store your apples in a dry, cool place until you're ready to eat them.

What Type of Apples to Look For

The types of apples you can pick vary based on what part of the country you're in, but here is a general guide to the kinds of apples you should be on the lookout for:

- **BEST APPLES FOR BAKING:** Honeycrisp, Granny Smith, Golden Delicious, Cortland, Empire, Jonathan

- **BEST APPLES FOR CIDER:** Fuji, Cortland, Gala, Winesap, McIntosh, Honeycrisp

- **BEST APPLES TO EAT RAW:** Granny Smith, Fuji, Jonagold, Cortland, Winesap

Cardamom Ginger Apple Butter

MAKES 8 CUPS [2.3 KG] | **PREP TIME** 15 MINUTES | **TOTAL TIME** 12 HOURS

SO, YOU'VE GONE APPLE PICKING for the season. Now what?

There are an incredible number of recipes you can create with your freshly picked apples. One of my all-time favorites is apple butter. You might be surprised at how versatile it is: You can spread it on toast, add it to sandwiches, put it in cocktails . . . you can really get creative here.

This recipe makes a cute hostess or housewarming gift, or give it to friends, neighbors, or your kids' teachers. Just package the apple butter in a mason jar, add a label (which you can easily buy at a craft store or make yourself), and tie it with a bow. Autumn in a jar!

I've opted for a bit of a twist to a classic apple butter by adding cardamom and ginger. Cardamom is one of the best spices for fall—it's warm, fragrant, and tastes heavenly in baked goods.

FOOD

INGREDIENTS

3½ lb [1.6 kg] apples (approximately 6 medium, any variety), peeled, cored, and cut into ¼ in [6 mm] slices

1½ cups [360 ml] apple cider

½ cup [100 g] packed light brown sugar

¼ cup [40 g] crystallized ginger, finely chopped

½ tsp salt

1 Tbsp cornstarch

¾ tsp ground cardamom

½ tsp ground cinnamon

½ tsp vanilla extract

1 Place the apples, cider, brown sugar, crystallized ginger, and salt in a large heavy-bottomed pot. Cook over medium heat for about 30 minutes or until the apples are soft.

2 Using an immersion blender, purée the mixture until smooth. Alternatively, spoon the mixture into a blender in batches and blend. Return the mixture to the pot after blending.

3 Once puréed, add the cornstarch, cardamom, cinnamon, and vanilla. Cook on low for 1 to 2 hours. The mixture will darken in color and thicken.

4 Let the mixture cool. Spoon into desired containers. Covered, in the refrigerator, the apple butter will keep for up to 3 weeks.

Apple Ring Pancakes with Salted Caramel Dipping Sauce

SERVES 4 TO 6 | **PREP TIME** 30 MINUTES | **TOTAL TIME** 40 MINUTES

APPLES FOR BREAKFAST? Always a great idea in the fall!

For the folks who crave a sweet treat in the morning, this is the ideal apple dish for you. I love that these Apple Ring Pancakes incorporate all my favorite fall things: apples, cinnamon, and brown sugar. Just add a cozy flannel, socks, and slippers, and you're in full fall mode.

FOOD

INGREDIENTS

Caramel Sauce

½ cup [100g] granulated sugar

½ cup [100 g] packed light brown sugar

4 Tbsp [55 g] unsalted butter, cut into pieces

½ cup [120 ml] heavy cream, warmed

1½ tsp salt

1 To make the caramel sauce: In a medium pot, combine the granulated sugar and the light brown sugar. Warm over medium heat until melted.

2 Using a wooden spoon or heat-resistant spatula, stir in the 4 Tbsp of butter, mixing constantly until the butter has fully melted and combined with the sugar. Let cook undisturbed for 1 to 2 minutes.

3 Slowly stir in the cream. Be aware that it will bubble when added. Keep stirring until the cream has fully mixed in. Allow the mixture to cook undisturbed for 1 to 2 minutes. The mixture will rise in the pot; keep a watchful eye so it doesn't boil over.

4 Remove from the heat and sprinkle the salt over the surface. Allow to cool slightly and give it a good stir. The sauce will thicken as it cools. Set aside.

continued

47

Apple Ring Pancakes

2 Tbsp unsalted butter, cut into pieces

2 large apples, such as Granny Smith
or another firm, tart apple, peeled,
cored, cut into ½ in [12 mm] rings

1 Tbsp granulated sugar

1 tsp ground cinnamon

1 cup [120 g] pancake mix

5 To make the apple ring pancakes: Heat a large skillet over medium-high heat. Melt the 2 Tbsp of butter. Add the apple rings and sauté, flipping them every so often, until they start to soften, about 5 minutes. Set aside. In a small bowl, mix together the granulated sugar and cinnamon. Sprinkle over the cooked apples.

6 Prepare the pancake mix according to package directions for 6 to 8 pancakes.

7 Heat a large skillet over medium-low heat. Spray with nonstick spray. Dredge each apple ring in pancake batter. Place in the skillet. Cook for about 2 minutes per side or until they're golden brown. Serve immediately with the warm caramel sauce.

FOOD

Apple Cider Doughnut Muffins

SERVES 6 TO 8 | **PREP TIME** 5 MINUTES | **TOTAL TIME** 35 MINUTES

MY FAVORITE PART ABOUT GOING TO THE LOCAL ORCHARD EACH YEAR? Picking up some apple cider doughnuts, of course! I don't know why they're so delicious, but they are.

I love this spin on the apple cider doughnut. These muffins are incredibly easy to make, the perfect combination of savory and sweet, and they will satisfy your craving just in case you can't make it to an apple orchard to get your doughnut fix. Buy some apple cider at the orchard or your local market, or make some yourself with apples you picked fresh off the tree. Bon appétit!

FOOD

INGREDIENTS

½ cup [120 ml] apple cider
1½ cups [210 g] all-purpose flour
¾ cup [150 g] sugar
1½ tsp baking powder
½ tsp kosher salt
2 tsp ground cinnamon
¼ tsp ground nutmeg
10 Tbsp [140 g] unsalted butter
1 medium egg, beaten
½ cup [120 ml] whole milk
1 tsp vanilla extract
¼ tsp ground cardamom

1 Preheat the oven to 350°F [180°C] with a rack positioned in the center of the oven. Grease a muffin tin with nonstick spray. (You can also use unsalted butter or paper baking cups if you prefer.)

2 In a small pot, bring the apple cider to a boil, then lower the heat to a simmer. Cook down the cider for 10 minutes or until the cider has reduced by half.

3 In a large bowl, whisk together the flour, ½ cup [100 g] of the sugar, the baking powder, salt, 1 tsp of the cinnamon, and the nutmeg.

4 Melt 5 Tbsp [70 g] of the butter in a microwave-safe bowl. In a medium bowl, mix together the melted butter, reduced cider, egg, milk, and vanilla.

5 Gently mix the dry ingredients into the wet

ingredients, stirring just until combined. Spoon the batter into the prepared muffin tin, filling the cups three-fourths of the way full.

6   Bake for 20 to 25 minutes, until the muffins have fully risen and start to turn golden brown. Allow to cool slightly in the pan.

7   Melt the remaining 5 Tbsp [70 g] of butter. In a small bowl, combine the remaining ¼ cup [50 g] of sugar, 1 tsp cinnamon, and the cardamom. Brush the top of each muffin with the butter and sprinkle with the sugar mixture. Serve immediately, or store covered at room temperature for up to 3 days.

Bourbon with Spiced Apple Shrub

SERVES 4 | **PREP TIME** 20 MINUTES | **TOTAL TIME** 30 MINUTES

SOMETHING ABOUT BOURBON JUST FEELS WARM AND SNUGGLY TO ME. Once the temperature dips, it's the spirit that I find myself reaching for most often. From mulled ciders to maple old-fashioneds, it's an ideal ingredient in a number of fall cocktails—including this one! After you've gone apple picking in September, this Bourbon with Spiced Apple Shrub cocktail is a great way to make use of all that freshly picked fruit you've gathered at your local orchard and (re)introduce bourbon into your bar cart!

What on earth is a shrub, you ask? In short: It's a bit of a beverage unicorn. A shrub is a sweet-tart, nonalcoholic syrup that is super versatile. It can be added to cocktails, served with club soda for an everyday sipper, or enjoyed on its own. When fall comes around, I love to use seasonal produce to make homemade shrubs. They're ideal for entertaining, and you can make so many different delicious drinks with them that cater to everyone in your circle.

INGREDIENTS

Spiced Apple Shrub

1 cup [200 g] sugar
2 medium apples, any variety,
    shredded with peel
4 to 6 black peppercorns
2 cardamom pods
1 cinnamon stick
½ vanilla bean
1 cup [240 ml] apple cider vinegar

1 To make the spiced apple shrub: In a medium pot, combine 1 cup [240 ml] of water with the sugar, shredded apple, peppercorns, cardamom pods, cinnamon stick, and vanilla bean. Bring to a boil over medium heat.

2 Once boiling, reduce heat to low and simmer for 15 minutes. Remove from the heat and mix in the apple cider vinegar. Let cool to room temperature. Strain, keeping the liquid and discarding the rest.

Cocktail

6 oz [180 ml] bourbon

4 oz [120 ml] Spiced Apple Shrub
   (recipe precedes)

4 oz [120 ml] apple cider

12 oz [360 ml] ginger ale

4 apple slices, for garnish

4 cinnamon sticks, for garnish

3 To make the cocktail: Place cubed ice in four rocks glasses. Set aside.

4 In a large cocktail shaker, add ½ cup [120 ml] of ice, the bourbon, spiced shrub, and apple cider. Give it a good shake for 10 to 20 seconds.

5 Strain equally over the rocks glasses. Top off each glass with 3 oz [90 ml] of the ginger ale. Garnish with an apple slice and cinnamon stick.

NOTE: *The shrub can be made ahead and stored in the refrigerator for up to 2 weeks.*

Sausage, Apple, and Root Vegetable Bake

SERVES 4 TO 6 | **PREP TIME** 30 MINUTES | **TOTAL TIME** 40 MINUTES

FOOD

AS I'VE GOTTEN OLDER, I've come to appreciate a good savory baked dish. It's easy for entertaining, or for nights when you just don't feel like preparing a meal with all the sides and frills. Which, for me, is almost every night, but I digress.

This Sausage, Apple, and Roasted Root Vegetable Bake is jam-packed with vegetables, which is pretty deceiving considering how delicious it is. It feels like a cheat meal, but it definitely isn't. This recipe is also another great way to use up those extra apples from your apple picking trip or your local farmers' market.

The best part about this recipe is that it's ready in less than an hour. This is a great dish for anyone on the go—no need to spend hours in the kitchen to create a veggie-packed meal.

INGREDIENTS

One 10 oz [285 g] package chicken apple sausage, cut into 1 in [2.5 cm] slices

3 carrots, peeled and sliced

2 apples, any variety, peeled and cut into 1 in [2.5 cm] slices

2 parsnips, peeled and sliced

1 small sweet potato, diced

1 yellow onion, thinly sliced

1 small rutabaga, peeled and finely diced

Olive oil

Kosher salt

Freshly ground black pepper

1 Preheat the oven to 475°F [240°C] with a rack positioned in the center of the oven.

2 Place the sausage, carrots, apples, parsnips, sweet potato, onion, and rutabaga in a large bowl, drizzle with olive oil until lightly coated, and season with salt and pepper. Give it a good stir to fully coat everything. Tip out onto a rimmed baking sheet.

3 Bake for 15 minutes, stir, and roast for another 15 minutes, or until the vegetables are fork-tender and beginning to brown. Let cool slightly and serve warm.

Apple Slab Pie

SERVES 14 TO 16 | **PREP TIME** 1 HOUR | **TOTAL TIME** 1 HOUR AND 40 MINUTES

IS IT REALLY AUTUMN if you haven't had apple pie? I think not.

    This Apple Slab Pie is an open-faced, easy, elegant pie that is sure to wow your friends and family. You're welcome to make the pie dough and apple butter for this pie from scratch, or if you're short on time, you can use premade apple butter and pie dough disks. No judgment.

FOOD

INGREDIENTS

1 cup [220 g] unsalted butter

2½ cups [300 g] all-purpose flour

1 Tbsp kosher salt

1 Tbsp ground ginger

1 Tbsp ground cinnamon

¼ tsp ground allspice

¼ tsp ground clove

1 cup [240 ml] ice water

1½ cups prepared apple butter [360 g], like the Cardamom Ginger Apple Butter on page 46

1 medium egg

3 lb [1.5 kg] apples (approximately 10 medium), any variety

1 Tbsp sugar

1 Cut the butter into small cubes and place in the freezer for about 5 minutes.

2 In a large bowl, whisk the flour, salt, ginger, 2 tsp of the cinnamon, allspice, and clove to combine.

3 Remove the butter from the freezer and add to the flour mixture. If you have naturally warm hands, wash your hands in cold water. Using your fingers, pinch each piece of butter to flatten and break them up into smaller pieces. Gently mix to coat all the butter pieces in flour. The butter pieces should be about the size of almonds.

4 Slowly, add about ¼ cup [60 ml] of ice water at a time to the flour. Stir gently, trying not to press or stir too hard. Let the water get fully absorbed before adding the next ¼ cup [60 ml]. Keep adding water and gently stirring by hand until the dough comes together. The total amount of water needed may vary based on the brand of flour used. If the dough seems too wet, add more flour, about 1 Tbsp at a time, until the dough is

the right consistency. The dough should not be sticky or crumbly but should easily come together and have visible pieces of butter throughout. Remove the dough from the bowl, shape into a disk, wrap in plastic wrap, and refrigerate for at least 30 minutes.

5 Preheat the oven to 425°F [220°] with an oven rack set in the center.

6 Once the pie dough has fully chilled, roll it into a 15 by 18 in [38 by 46 cm] rectangle. Place the pie dough into an ungreased 9 by 13 in [23 by 33 cm] pan. Cover the dough with parchment paper and add pie weights or dried beans up to the rim of the dish to weight down the crust as it bakes. Bake for 20 minutes, remove the parchment paper, and bake for an additional 5 minutes. Let cool.

7 Mix the apple butter with the egg and spread over the bottom of the cooled pie crust.

8 Peel, core, and thinly slice the apples. Neatly arrange the apple slices over the apple butter so they're slightly overlapping. Sprinkle with the sugar and remaining 1 tsp of cinnamon.

9 Bake for approximately 35 minutes or until the crust is golden brown and the filling is beginning to bubble. Let cool on a metal rack for 30 minutes before cutting and serving.

NOTES: *For this recipe you'll need a 9 by 13 in [23 by 33 cm] pan. Also, this recipe calls for prepared apple butter. The Cardamom Ginger Apple Butter on page 46 works very well with this recipe, or feel free to use store-bought. As part of this recipe, I've included a ginger spice–flavored pie dough. If you're intimidated by making pie dough from scratch, feel free to substitute regular pie dough for the spiced dough by using two premade pie dough disks. Simply unroll and stack the crusts one on top of the other. Roll into a 15 by 18 in [38 by 46 cm] rectangle, refrigerate, and start at step 6.*

FOOD

October

I DON'T LIKE TO PICK FAVORITES, but there's something incredibly special about the month of October. The air is crisp. You can always detect a hint of woodsmoke in the air (or am I just imagining that?). The leaves are changing. You get to experience autumn foliage in all its glory. As Albert Camus once said, "Autumn is a second spring when every leaf is a flower."

The theme for this month is *play*. Remember what it was like to be a kid and get dressed up in a costume, play make-believe, go trick-or-treating, and eat ALL of the candy? It was the best time of the year! Recreate that childish joy all month long with the nostalgic activities that October has to offer. From DIY Halloween crafts and haunted houses to leaf-peeping trips and pumpkin patch visits with family or friends, there are plenty of ways to make the most of the season and this remarkable month.

One thing you should absolutely do in October? Take advantage of all things pumpkin. Carve them, pile them on your stoop, create cool pumpkin-themed crafts, craft a boozy pumpkin spice latte, and/or cook all kinds of tasty pumpkin recipes. Whatever you do, stock up on pumpkins this month to make your home feel as cozy and festive as possible.

Not to mention it's the start of spooky season! Whether you go all out for Halloween with a homemade costume and a big party or prefer snuggling at home and having a scary movie marathon, here you'll find plenty of ideas and ways to celebrate one of the greatest holidays.

From leaf-peeping to PSLs to Halloween, let's get to it and make this the best month of the year!

Leaf-Peeping

ACTIVITY

LET'S FACE IT: New England in the fall is pretty magical. But what if I told you that there are so many other picturesque places to visit around the country with gorgeous fall foliage?

If you're planning a leaf-peeping adventure this fall, here are five places outside of New England that should be on your radar.

Hudson Valley, New York

In the Hudson Valley, you can begin your leaf-peeping journey in the beautiful historic town of Rhinebeck, located just north of New York City. It is known for its historic charm and is home to America's oldest continuously operating inn. Here, you'll find miles and miles of meadowland, streams, and wooded hills with stunning mountain vistas across the Hudson River.

From there, you can head up to the bucolic town of Hudson with its outstanding restaurants, cross the river and experience the charm of Kingston, or head south on Route 9 to Beacon and visit some of the best art galleries, breweries, and distilleries in the country. You won't want to miss the Storm King Art Center either—here, you can gaze upon large-scale artwork nestled into the beautiful fall landscape.

Blue Ridge Parkway, Virginia and North Carolina

Driving the Blue Ridge Parkway should 100 percent be on your bucket list. And if you can do it in the fall, it's even better. This 469 mile [755 km] highway is a slow-paced and relaxing drive in the heart of the Blue Ridge Mountains. Whether you drive the entire length of it or pop in on certain cities, be sure to have your camera ready for all the stunning scenic overlooks.

The Blue Ridge Parkway begins at US 250 in Rockfish Gap, Virginia, which is located right outside of Charlottesville, Virginia. Begin your journey in Virginia Wine Country,

ACTIVITY

visit some world-class wineries and restaurants in town, and hop on the parkway to enjoy some of the beautiful fall colors.

You can take the Blue Ridge Parkway all the way from Charlottesville, Virginia, to Asheville, North Carolina, if you'd like. Asheville is a quirky town full of charm, character, and plenty of hiking trails, and is one of the country's top destinations for craft breweries.

Guadalupe Mountains National Park, Texas

Fall in Texas? You wouldn't expect it, but it exists! The Guadalupe Mountains National Park is for the true fall adventurer. A long drive from everywhere, it is seldom busy.

By visiting this slower-paced national park, you can take in nature at your own speed with hardly anyone or anything to bother you. There is no lodging available inside the park, but you can book a bed-and-breakfast either in Dell City, Texas, or Whites City, New Mexico, for easy access. Take on some of the most beautiful fall hikes in the park such as the McKittrick Canyon Trail or the Smith Spring Trail and immerse yourself in nature and glorious fall foliage.

Mount Laguna and Julian, California

Just an hour outside of San Diego, Mount Laguna is a California fall lover's paradise, with expansive views of the large pines that cover the Cleveland National Forest. To make it feel like a classic fall outing, continue a little farther north to the town of Julian, an old gold-mining town that now has some of the best apple picking in the state. Julian is famous for their apple pie, so make sure to grab a slice before you hit the road.

Columbia River Gorge, Oregon

Columbia River Gorge is a picturesque stretch of canyon along the Columbia River in the Pacific Northwest. To experience the foliage in a unique way, visit Multnomah Falls, a gorgeous 600 foot [183 m] waterfall. You can view the fall foliage from the bottom of the waterfall, or, if you're looking for a stunning midlevel vantage point, head to the iconic Benson Bridge and let the surroundings immerse you in fall colors.

Timeless Sweaters

FOR FALL

WHILE FALL TRENDS COME AND GO, there's one staple you can bank on season after season: the timeless sweater.

Don't we all love sweater weather? There's something so inviting about this time of year when temperatures have cooled down, the air is brisk, the leaves are falling, and you're curled up drinking a hot cider.

Instead of opting for the season's trendiest fall sweaters, start a capsule wardrobe with classic sweaters that will look great year after year. If you're sweater shopping this season, here are some solid bets that will never go out of style.

- **A TURTLENECK SWEATER:** For those extra chilly days when you need a bit more coverage, turtleneck sweaters will always do the trick and will transition into winter with ease. It's up to you if you want thick or thin fabric, a boxy or fitted shape. I'd recommend

scooping up a few of these in festive fall colors such as rust and oxblood to pair with your favorite fall bottoms or pair of jeans.

- **A CASHMERE CREWNECK SWEATER:** You can't go wrong with a crewneck cashmere sweater. It's classic, pairs well with a lot of pieces, and is flattering on most body types. Plus, there are plenty of clothing brands that offer cashmere at more affordable price points nowadays, so it has become way more attainable in recent years.

- **THE FISHERMAN SWEATER:** These sweaters, originally known as Aran sweaters, first appeared in the late 1800s or early 1900s. They take their name from the Aran Islands off the Irish coast, which are surrounded by freezing cold seas and often experience gloomy weather. These sweaters were designed to keep farmers and fishermen as warm as possible (hence their common name, fisherman sweaters). Since the sweaters were made from unadulterated lambswool, they were typically cream colored. The women of the islands made them using intricate cable and knot-like stitching, and one sweater could take up to two months to make. After *Vogue* posted a photo of Grace Kelly wearing a fisherman sweater in 1950, it became a worldwide trend and an instant classic.

- **A CARDIGAN:** Layering is key in the fall. It might be chilly in the morning only to be warm in the afternoon, so sometimes, you'll want a sweater that you can easily take off and put on at a moment's notice. Enter: the classic cardigan. This evergreen sweater was named after James Brudenell, 7th Earl of Cardigan, who was a British army major general. Supposedly, Brudenell invented the

garment to keep warm on the battlefield. Coco Chanel popularized the cardigan and reinvented it for women in the 1920s, and it has been a closet staple ever since.

DIY Leaf Photo Wall

LOOKING TO ADD A LITTLE SPICE to your fall photos? Try making this super simple DIY leaf wall for the perfect seasonal photo shoot!

A leaf wall is a fantastic, simple craft idea that you can do with friends or family. It makes a great backdrop for photos of your family or pets, for a "photo booth" at a party, or even for video calls!

MATERIALS AND TOOLS

Foam board: Find these at your local craft store and get the largest one you think you'll need to cover the entire background of your photo. Tip: Take a picture with your phone or camera in-store to get a sense of how big of a board you'll need to purchase.

Glue: A hot glue gun is preferred, but an all-purpose liquid glue can work in a pinch.

Leaves: You can use colored leaves found on the ground or buy bags of fake leaves from your local craft store or online.

X-Acto knife (optional)

1 Make sure the foam board is clean and has no debris before starting. Using the glue, adhere the leaves to the foam board, ensuring there is even and full coverage across the entire board.

2 After your first layer of leaves are glued and dried to the foam core, add additional leaves on top of that layer to create depth in your background. Do this as many times as you'd like.

3 Optional: After taking all the images you want in front of the wall, take an X-Acto knife and cut a small circle out of the center of the board. With this cutout, you can then stick various things through the hole and take creative shots. Start with a small circle, and expand it as needed.

Some photo ideas with different-size cutouts include:

- Pet-size cutout for your furry family member— stick their head through the hole!
- Child-size for a silly portrait that kids will love
- Adult-size for a fun portrait of you
- Multiple holes for a creative family photo

DECOR & DIY

Gold Leaf Pumpkin Art

WHILE CARVING PUMPKINS IS FUN, it's definitely not an activity for everyone. Between the heavy lifting, the cleanup, and the fact that a pumpkin will rot a few days after carving, it's sometimes not the ideal pumpkin craft of the season.

Enter: the painted gold leaf pumpkin. What I love about this craft is that it majorly elevates your space, you can craft these to match your home decor with ease, and the cleanup hardly takes any time at all. Plus, this will last a lot longer than a carved pumpkin—most years, the pumpkin will keep all the way to Thanksgiving.

If you're short on time and want to cut down on the number of supplies for this DIY, try drawing some patterns on a white pumpkin with a gold leaf pen.

MATERIALS AND TOOLS

Pumpkins
Parchment paper or newspaper to protect work surface
Two 1 in [2.5 cm] flat paintbrushes
Metal leaf adhesive
Gold metal leaf sheets
Soft bristle brush

1 Make sure your pumpkin is clean and free of dirt or smudges before you begin. Place a piece of parchment on your work surface to protect it.

2 Dip the tip of your paintbrush in the metal leaf adhesive. Brush the adhesive onto the top of your pumpkin, working slightly down each segment of the pumpkin. Allow the adhesive to dry thoroughly. The adhesive should go on white, and when dry, it will be tacky and clear.

3 Carefully lay a piece of gold metal leaf on top of the pumpkin and use a clean paintbrush to gently press it against the adhesive. Work very gently with the gold leaf, as it breaks easily.

4 Use the soft bristle brush to press the gold leaf into the adhesive and burnish it. The gold leaf will flake off wherever there is not adhesive. You can also use the palm of your hand to burnish the gold leaf. Repeat step 2 if you make any holes in the gold leaf while brushing.

5 Repeat steps 3 and 4 until you have covered all the adhesive on the pumpkin.

Spooky Halloween Decor

I DON'T BELIEVE IN SPENDING a ton of money on Halloween decor. You can easily make a lot of decor yourself, and with items that you already have at home.

If you're looking to get into the spooky spirit this year, here are five Halloween decor pieces you can create in the comfort of your own home.

Spiderwebs

You can buy faux spiderwebs at any party store for not too much money, but you can also easily make them yourself using cotton balls.

Take a bunch of cotton balls and stretch them out. Use hairspray to attach the stretched-out cotton balls together. Continue stretching out the cotton balls and piecing them together with hairspray until the web is at the desired size. Hang the web with white thumbtacks, and add small plastic spiders, if you wish!

Mummify Your Door

This is a cute and easy DIY that you can do with your whole family. Cut strips of white crepe paper or use white streamers to wrap your door, crisscrossing the paper or streamers as you go and adhering them to your door with adhesive putty. Trim any excess and add a large set of googly eyes to the paper on the front side of your door using adhesive putty or a hot glue gun.

Bat Wall

This bat wall DIY is very budget-friendly yet looks incredibly chic! For this project, you'll need white printer paper, scissors, black cardstock, and painter's tape or adhesive putty. Trace the outline of a bat (either drawn freehand or find an image online to trace) on your white piece of paper, and cut it out to create your template. Create bat templates of varying sizes to make this project more dimensional. Place the template(s) over the

black cardstock and cut out the outline. Adhere the bats to your wall using painter's tape or putty. I like to tape the bats in a diagonal pattern, but the placement is completely up to you.

DIY Black Candlesticks

Have some old wine bottles lying around? Turn them into fun and festive decor! For this project you'll need an empty wine bottle (or several—an assortment of shapes and sizes would be fun), black all-surface spray paint, and taper candles. Make sure to remove any labels from the wine bottles and wash them to remove any debris or residue. Allow the bottles to dry completely. Place the bottles in a well-ventilated area on a protective surface and spray-paint the bottles. You'll need two or three coats; give yourself 30 minutes in between coats to allow the bottles to dry. Allow the bottles at least 24 hours to dry fully. Place your taper candles in your new DIY candlesticks—black, white, gold, or silver candlesticks look best.

Coffee Can Ghosts

This is a fantastic way to upcycle some of the used cans you might have hanging around your house. Plus, it's easy and the ghosts are adorable!

For this project, you'll need a few cans (coffee cans work well, but any cans will do), white spray paint, a permanent marker, scissors, a hot glue gun, white streamers, and twine. Remove any labels from the cans and wash the cans to remove any debris. When the cans are fully dry, head to a well-ventilated area and spray-paint the cans on a protective surface. You'll need two or three coats; give yourself 30 minutes in between coats to allow the cans to dry. Allow the cans at least 24 hours to dry fully.

When the cans are dry, draw a set of eyes and a mouth on each can with the permanent marker. Cut six to eight streamers of equal length and attach them to the inside of the cans with the hot glue gun so the streamers hang through the open end of the can. On the top part of the can, use a knife to carefully punch two holes and string some twine through to hang the can. These ghostly friends look great outside hanging from a trellis, a porch overhang, or tree branches.

HOW TO STYLE A
Halloween Bar Cart

I'M A FIRM BELIEVER in having fun with your bar cart from season to season. One of my favorite times of year to style my bar cart is Halloween. It's a great focal point for your space, ideal for entertaining, and a good way to style the five too many mini pumpkins you purchased at the pumpkin patch.

I also love a good Halloween bar cart because it gives me a chance to use spooky decor in a chic way. Don't get me wrong, I love Halloween, but I don't want my entire home looking like a haunted house—but if that's your thing, go all out! Here's where you can be creative, add cheeky accents, and get in the festive spirit.

First things first: Choose a color scheme. I love adding metallic and black accents to my Halloween bar cart to make it seem a bit more elevated and luxe. For the top level of the bar cart, display a few of the ingredients necessary to create your signature drink. (With my black-and-metallic bar cart, I'll typically do a Spooky French 75 cocktail; see recipe on page 81.) Consider pairing spooky elements such as decorative skulls or spiders with sweet elements like cute straws or a bowl of candy for guests.

Keep the stylized "overflow"—extra glasses for guests, shakers, and other cocktail paraphernalia—on the bottom of the cart. If you have any fun glassware that goes with your theme (for example, I'll grab a few of my favorite black and white coffee mugs to go with the black-and-metallic theme), add those to the cart's bottom, along with more festive elements like mini pumpkins and skeletons from a craft store.

Here are three different Halloween-themed palettes with bar cart recipes to choose from, or to inspire you to create your own. All in all, have fun styling your Halloween bar cart. I like to put mine together in early October so that I'm in the spooky season mood all month long.

DECOR & DIY

Black, Silver, and Gold

- 5 to 7 mini pumpkins spray-painted black, silver, and gold
- 12 to 15 gold votive candles
- Gold or silver streamers (to hang from or above your bar cart)
- Black spiders (webs optional)
- Black and gold straws
- Spooky French 75 ingredients (see page 81)
- Champagne flutes
- White and black coffee mugs

Orange and White

- 5 to 7 mini white and orange pumpkins
- Orange-and-white striped straws
- Bowl of candy corn
- Paper ghost garland
- Mimosa ingredients: champagne and orange juice
- Sliced oranges for garnish
- Champagne flutes

Purple and Green

- 5 to 7 mini white pumpkins, spray-painted purple and green
- Purple striped straws
- Bowl of green M&M's
- A witch's hat and/or a green goblin's hand
- Plenty of purple and green ribbons in different widths and styles, amassed together and strung up along the edge of the bar cart like bunting
- A bottle of absinthe
- Coupe glasses

DECOR & DIY

Spooky French 75

SERVES 4 | **PREP TIME** 5 MINUTES | **TOTAL TIME** 5 MINUTES

THE BEST WAY TO CELEBRATE spooky season is with a festive cocktail. And I'll let you in on a little secret: I've made a lot of my favorite cocktails "spooky" by adding activated charcoal. It makes your drink look as dark as night, or like a witch's brew, but it will still taste delicious! Plus, if you're not feeling so hot the day after Halloween, activated charcoal is great to have on hand to help you bounce back—it's considered a potent natural detox treatment.

I love this Spooky French 75 because it looks incredibly elegant and elevated, but it's super simple to make at home. Gin and champagne are a classic duo (the French 75 dates back to as early as 1915), and the activated charcoal brings it into the twenty-first century.

DRINK

INGREDIENTS

8 oz [240 ml] London dry gin
3 oz [90 ml] fresh lemon juice
3 oz [90 ml] simple syrup
⅛ tsp activated charcoal
8 oz [240 ml] champagne
4 long orange twists, for garnish

1 In a large cocktail shaker, combine the gin, lemon juice, simple syrup, and activated charcoal. Add a handful of ice, cover, and shake for about 20 seconds.

2 Strain equally into four champagne flutes, top each glass with 2 oz [60 ml] of the champagne, and garnish with an orange twist.

The Ultimate Halloween Party Playlist

THERE ARE SOME SERIOUSLY CATCHY SPOOKY SEASON JAMS out there that I encourage you to play all October long. They're fun, festive, and may or may not get stuck in your head. If you're hosting a Halloween party this year, or if you're just looking to get into the spooky spirit, here is the ultimate playlist. Jam out to oldies, classic songs, and modern bops—whatever your music preference! →

Best Songs for Your Halloween Playlist

- **"HALLOWEEN THEME" JOHN CARPENTER**–It's creepy, it's classic, and it will start your party off with a bang. Even though the slasher franchise has eleven movies to its name, you can't beat the original soundtrack.

- **"STRANGER THINGS" KYLE DIXON AND MICHAEL STEIN**–When *Stranger Things* debuted on Netflix in 2016, it was an instant classic. And the theme song perfectly matches the spooky energy of this acclaimed series.

- **"BLACK MAGIC WOMAN" FLEETWOOD MAC**–Santana's cover of this 1969 classic might be more well known, but you'll be jamming to the original version of this song all night long.

- **"MONSTER MASH" BOBBY "BORIS" PICKETT**–Name a more iconic Halloween song. I'll wait.

- **"DING DONG! THE WITCH IS DEAD" ELLA FITZGERALD**– Ella Fitzgerald's jazzy, upbeat cover of the popular song from *The Wizard of Oz* is a must-listen.

- **"MAIN THEME: THE ADDAMS FAMILY" VIC MIZZY**– Naturally, the theme song from this classic spooky show is a perfect fit for your Halloween playlist.

- **"THIS IS HALLOWEEN" THE CITIZENS OF HALLOWEEN**– This classic song from *The Nightmare Before Christmas* is likely to get stuck in your head.

- **"TIME WARP" LITTLE NELL, PATRICIA QUINN, AND RICHARD O'BRIEN**– This bop from *The Rocky Horror Picture Show* will get your guests on the dance floor.

- **"GHOSTBUSTERS" RAY PARKER JR.**–One of the most iconic movies of the '80s has a pretty iconic theme song to go along with it.

- **"SOMEBODY'S WATCHING ME" ROCKWELL**–Who hasn't belted out this classic whenever a pet or a human looks at you for a little too long?

- **"I PUT A SPELL ON YOU" NINA SIMONE**–Bette Midler has a pretty incredible cover of this song for *Hocus Pocus*, but the original version is just as catchy.

- **"SUPERSTITION" STEVIE WONDER**–OK, let's be real. You aren't going to get 7 years of bad luck, but on Halloween, you might feel that way. This snappy song will bring you back to reality.

- **"ZOMBIE" THE CRANBERRIES**–This quintessential '90s bop written by Dolores O'Riordan will inevitably spark an epic alt-rock sing-along at your next fête.

- **"CREEP" RADIOHEAD**– Is it really Halloween if you aren't a little creeped out? I think not.

- **"HIGHWAY TO HELL" AC/DC**–Is it really Halloween if you don't scream this song at the top of your lungs? Again, I think not.

- **"SCARY MONSTERS (AND SUPER CREEPS)" DAVID BOWIE**–The title says it all. This is one of David Bowie's most underrated songs.

- **"THRILLER" MICHAEL JACKSON**–Dare I say this might be the best Halloween jam of all time? If you want to go above and beyond, you can attempt to learn the choreography from the music video and recreate it at your party!

- **"A NIGHTMARE ON MY STREET" DJ JAZZY JEFF & THE FRESH PRINCE**–In case you needed a reminder that Will Smith had a robust music career before he got into acting, this is a wholesome song by the dynamic duo from Philadelphia.

- **"MONSTER" KANYE WEST FEATURING JAY-Z, RICK ROSS, NICKI MINAJ, AND BON IVER**–This smash hit song undoubtedly contains one of Nicki Minaj's best verses of all time.

- **"DISTURBIA" RIHANNA**–I'm not sure if Rihanna is really scaring anyone with this song, but I can guarantee you one thing: It will get stuck in your head.

- **"HAUNTED" BEYONCÉ**– A pretty experimental song from Beyoncé that will match any spooky vibe to a T.

- **"MONSTER" LADY GAGA**– There's a reason Lady Gaga calls her fans "Little Monsters"—she's one of the resident queens of spooky.

- **"HEADS WILL ROLL" YEAH YEAH YEAHS**–Who knew a spooky song about decapitation could be so darn catchy?

- **"MANEATER" NELLY FURTADO**–If there's ever a zombie apocalypse, this song will come in handy: Nelly Furtado predicts how to spot a maneater in this bop.

- **"SPOOKY, SCARY SKELETONS (UNDEAD TOMBSTONE REMIX)" ANDREW GOLD**–You'll want to party all night to this fun remix.

Halloween Party Activities

ACTIVITY

SO, YOU'VE GOT THE MENU ALL SET, your perfect DIY costume ready, and the decor is just right. The only thing left to make your Halloween party one for the books is to have an evening filled with fun activities for your guests to enjoy (if eating and sipping on cocktails isn't enough)! Here are some simple ideas to entertain your guests at your Halloween shindig.

Pumpkin Carving Contest

If you've got the space in your home or backyard and are down for a bit of cleanup, a pumpkin carving competition is quintessential for Halloween. Have your guests carve a design into a pumpkin of their choice, and let your guests vote on the best pumpkin.

To make a pumpkin carving contest run smoothly, you can purchase premade carving kits, which will have a good saw and a sturdy scooper. Make sure to get pumpkins that are large and have a smooth side for easier carving. Also, use flameless, battery-operated candles to keep everyone at the party safe.

Don't forget the newspaper! This will make cleanup much easier.

Eat a Doughnut off a String

This is a great way to engage Halloween party guests of all ages. It's a very easy game to set up, and your guests will appreciate the sweet treats.

All you need are doughnuts, string, and a pole or broomstick to set this game up. If you can get your hands on apple cider doughnuts, even better!

Tie your doughnuts with a piece of string, then attach the string to a pole or broomstick. Have a race to see which guest can eat the doughnut the fastest—without hands. Take turns trying to eat the doughnuts and holding the pole. You'll have just as much fun on either side of the game!

Costume Competition

A costume contest is a great way to get all your attendees in the festive spirit. After all, who doesn't like a little competition?

How you structure the contest is completely up to you. You can judge individuals, families, or couples—this just depends on who's attending the party. Create a few voting categories and ask your guests to vote on their favorite costumes once it gets toward the end of the night.

Some costume categories include:

- Scariest
- Most Original
- Best Couples
- Cutest
- Best Handmade
- Funniest
- Best Overall

Pin the Tail on the Cat

This game is silly enough for kids but entertaining enough for adults as well. The concept is simple: It's a twist on pin the tail on the donkey. Instead of the donkey, you have a black cat, which is perfect for Halloween.

Hang your tail-less cat on a wall. (You can cut the cat out of black cardstock and/or look for a template online.) Blindfold each guest, hand them a "tail," then spin them around until they are disoriented. The guest should try to correctly place the tail on the cat. You're bound to get plenty of misses and laughs, and it's a fun and festive way to celebrate the evening.

Guess How Many Candy Corn

For math enthusiasts, this is the ideal Halloween activity.

Before the party, place candy corn (or whatever candy of choice!) in a jar, counting the pieces as you fill it. At the party, have your guests guess how many pieces of candy are in the jar. Create little slips of paper for your guests to write their name and their guess. Next to the candy jar, place the blank slips of paper, a few pens, an empty bowl or jar to put the guesses in, and a sign explaining the game. Announce the winner at the end of the event. The winner can go home with the jar of candy, and/or you could sweeten the deal and come up with a separate or additional prize.

WATCH IT!

The Best Scary Movies

HAVE YOU EVER NOTICED HOW UNFORGETTABLE a classic Halloween film can be? They seem to never age, and I can watch them regularly with delight. Some are downright scary, while others inspire a bit of a chuckle.

As the leaves fall and the temperatures cool down in October, usher in the spooky season by enjoying a night at home and rewatching some of these classics. You can watch these films on your own, with friends (either in-person or during a virtual movie night), or with a loved one to get in the spirit of the season. Don't forget the seasonal snacks!! ➜

Top Ten Classic Films for Halloween

- **CASPER (1995)** – Looking for a somewhat dark yet family-friendly Halloween film? Casper is a twelve-year-old friendly ghost who wanders a home for over 100 years before finally finding friendship.

- **DOUBLE, DOUBLE, TOIL AND TROUBLE (1993)** – This classic film stars everyone's favorite '90s twins, Mary-Kate and Ashley Olsen, and follows them as they try to break their aunt free from an evil curse.

- **GET OUT (2017)** – The most recent film on this list, but an instant classic. *Get Out* is a brilliant psychological thriller that adds much-needed diversity and representation in the horror film world.

- **HALLOWEENTOWN (1998)** – Another '90s classic, but this one follows a young witch who's navigating the enchanted land of her grandmother, where it's Halloween all the time.

- **HOCUS POCUS (1993)** – I love to kick off the month of October by rewatching the classic film *Hocus Pocus*. It's a lighthearted Disney film that stars Sarah Jessica Parker, Bette Midler, and Kathy Najimy as resurrected witches from Salem, Massachusetts, and is packed with funny moments and memorable lines.

- **THE NIGHTMARE BEFORE CHRISTMAS (1993)** – Is it a Halloween movie? Is it a Christmas flick? Well, it's a little bit of both: Follow Jack Skellington, the king of Halloween Town, as he makes his way to Christmas Town.

- **THE ROCKY HORROR PICTURE SHOW (1975)** – Fun fact: This musical is the longest-running theatrical release in history. This cult-classic film is an absolute must. Many movie theaters across the United States screen *The Rocky Horror Picture Show* around Halloween, so grab some friends, head to a local showing, and make a night out of it!

- **SCREAM (1996)** – *Scream* is certain to give you plenty of entertainment. It's jam-packed with some of the biggest stars of the '90s and is truly timeless.

- **THE SILENCE OF THE LAMBS (1991)** – You might want to sleep with a night-light after watching this classic film about an FBI agent chasing down a serial killer.

- **PSYCHO (1960)** – Can you name a more iconic horror film? I think not! Alfred Hitchcock's signature style of filmmaking has been admired in Hollywood for decades, and this film is a must-see.

ACTIVITY

Pumpkin Pecan Granola

SERVES 6 TO 8 | **PREP TIME** 5 MINUTES | **TOTAL TIME** 35 MINUTES

GRANOLA IS LOW-KEY AN MVP INGREDIENT, and I think it's incredibly underrated. Just think about it: Have you really used granola to its fullest potential in your kitchen?

- Add granola to your seasonal salads to lend a fantastic, crunchy texture.

- Make a trail mix. Combine granola, dried fruit, nuts, and some cereal or chocolate chips for a snack you can enjoy on the go.

- Use granola as a substitute for bread crumbs. This works especially well for stuffing!

- Sprinkle granola on top of your ice cream for a delicious dessert.

- Mix granola into your muffin, brownie, cake, or pancake batter for an unexpected crunch.

While it's super easy to pick up a granola at the store, it's also very simple to make your own granola at home. I love the seasonal twist of this dish in particular: the pumpkin, pecan, and dried cranberries all balance each other out perfectly, and create a delicious burst of fall flavors in your mouth.

continued

FOOD

INGREDIENTS

4 cups [400 g] old-fashioned oats

1½ cups [180 g] raw pecans

⅔ cup [40 g] pepitas

1 tsp kosher salt

½ tsp pumpkin pie spice

½ tsp ground cinnamon

½ cup [150 g] pumpkin purée

½ cup [170 g] honey

⅓ cup [75 g] coconut oil, melted

1 tsp vanilla extract

1 Tbsp sugar

⅔ cup [90 g] dried cranberries

1 Preheat the oven to 325°F [170°C] with a rack positioned in the center of the oven. Line a rimmed baking sheet with parchment paper.

2 In a large bowl, combine the oats, pecans, pepitas, ½ tsp of the salt, the pie spice, and the cinnamon. Then add the pumpkin purée, honey, coconut oil, and vanilla. Stir gently to fully combine.

3 Tip out the granola mix onto the prepared pan. Gently spread out and press the granola into the tray. Sprinkle with the sugar and the remaining ½ tsp of salt.

4 Bake for 15 minutes, add the cranberries to the granola and give it a quick stir, rotate the tray, and bake for an additional 10 to 15 minutes. The granola should turn golden brown.

5 Let cool completely before breaking into pieces. Store in an airtight container at room temperature for up to 2 weeks.

Spiked Pumpkin Spice Latte with Oat Milk

SERVES 2 | **PREP TIME** 5 MINUTES | **TOTAL TIME** 10 MINUTES

AH, THE PSL. A staple of fall. I'm not going to lie: It might be considered a bit "basic" by some, but this beverage brings back a lot of memories for me. I've been enjoying some version of it for almost two decades now, and I've slowly but surely perfected my at-home PSLs over time.

Since I grew up with this beverage, I knew I wanted to make a boozy version of my beloved fall drink for this book. You're welcome to skip the alcohol if that's not your jam, or add more sugar if you want a sweeter PSL.

INGREDIENTS

1 cup [240 ml] pumpkin spice brewed coffee
½ cup [120 ml] oat milk
2 Tbsp pumpkin purée
1 Tbsp sugar
1 tsp vanilla extract
2 oz [60 ml] RumChata
1½ oz [45 ml] Fireball whisky

1 To serve warm, combine all the ingredients except the alcohol in a small pot and heat over medium-low heat. Stir until the pumpkin purée has fully dissolved and the mixture is warmed through, then add the alcohol and divide between two mugs.

2 To serve iced, place all the ingredients in a cocktail shaker with a few ice cubes. Shake until fully combined. Strain into two glasses filled with ice.

NOTE: *This recipe calls for pumpkin spice brewed coffee. If you don't have pumpkin spice coffee, and you do drip or French press, simply add pumpkin pie spice on top of the ground coffee and brew as you normally would. I use about 1 tsp for every ¼ cup [21 g] of ground coffee.*

This recipe can also be scaled up for a crowd and served warm in a slow cooker.

Homemade Pumpkin Butter

MAKES 4 CUPS [1.15 KG] | **PREP TIME** 5 MINUTES | **TOTAL TIME** 30 MINUTES

I DIDN'T REALIZE HOW MUCH I needed pumpkin butter during the fall until someone convinced me to buy it at the supermarket a few years ago. Now, fall just doesn't seem to be complete without it.

You can use pumpkin butter in so many ways. I love putting it on my waffles, English muffins, Greek yogurt, rolls, and baked goods . . . you name it, you can add pumpkin butter to it!

It is surprisingly simple to make pumpkin butter at home, plus I think it's a great gift for loved ones during the season. Just place it in a mason jar, tie a ribbon around it, and voilà! A small yet adorable token of gratitude.

FOOD

INGREDIENTS

3 cups [900 g] canned pumpkin

¾ cup [180 ml] apple cider

½ cup [100 g] packed dark
   brown sugar

¼ cup [85 g] maple syrup

½ tsp ground cinnamon

½ tsp kosher salt

¼ tsp pumpkin pie spice

1 Combine all the ingredients in a large heavy-bottomed pot. Stir and bring to a boil over medium-high heat.

2 Reduce the heat to low and simmer for approximately 25 minutes while stirring frequently. The pumpkin butter is done when the mixture has darkened in color and reduced by about half.

3 Let cool completely and store in airtight containers in the refrigerator for up to 2 weeks.

Pumpkin Biscuits

MAKES 6 TO 8 BISCUITS | **PREP TIME** 15 MINUTES | **TOTAL TIME** 30 MINUTES

MAYBE IT'S BECAUSE I WAS RAISED by a Southern woman, but something about biscuits just feels like home to me. Anyone else? It's a comfort food that's been with me through the good, the bad, and . . . yup, even the college years of my life.

These biscuits will certainly give you that at-home sensation, with a fun fall twist. They're fluffy, flaky, and perfect for breakfast or brunch. They taste great with honey or when used to create a breakfast sandwich. If you're feeling fancy, you can also use these biscuits as a base for your eggs Benedict.

INGREDIENTS

4 Tbsp [55 g] unsalted butter

2 cups [225 g] self-rising flour

1 Tbsp light brown sugar

½ tsp salt

¼ tsp pumpkin pie spice

½ cup [150 g] canned pumpkin

¼ cup [60 ml] milk, plus 2 to 3 Tbsp more as needed

1 Preheat the oven to 450°F [230°C] with a rack positioned in the center of the oven. Cut the butter into 1 in [2.5 cm] cubes and place in the freezer for 5 minutes.

2 In a large bowl, mix together the flour, brown sugar, salt, and pie spice, and brown sugar. Add the cold butter to the flour mixture. Using your hands, pinch the butter and mix into the flour until all the butter pieces are coated in flour and are about the size of peas.

3 Add the pumpkin and ¼ cup [60 ml] of the milk to the flour mixture, using your hands or a rubber spatula to gently mix and press the dough together about five times. If the dough seems too dry, add milk 1 Tbsp at a time, mixing two to three times before adding another.

4 Lightly flour a clean surface. Tip the biscuit dough onto the floured surface. Dust the dough with 1 Tbsp of flour, then roll the dough to approximately ½ in [12 mm] thick.

5 Use a round cutter or a water glass to press into the dough, but try not to twist the cutter. Place each biscuit onto an ungreased baking sheet at least 2 in [5 cm] apart. If desired, the dough can be rerolled one time to cut more biscuits.

6 Bake the biscuits for about 12 minutes until golden on top and around the edges. Serve warm.

FOOD

Curry Pumpkin Soup

SERVES 6 | **PREP TIME** 10 MINUTES | **TOTAL TIME** 30 MINUTES

FALL IS THE PERFECT TIME to experiment with all the spices. Curry powder typically contains turmeric, cumin, and cinnamon, which are all ideal flavors for fall. Any sweetness from the pumpkin will balance out the spicy curry flavor perfectly!

This dish is incredibly easy to make and is a great quick dinner option. If you're looking for a wine pairing, an off-dry Riesling is the perfect complement: The sweet wine will help tame some of the hot flavors in the curry.

FOOD

INGREDIENTS

2 Tbsp olive oil

1 medium yellow onion, finely diced

3 large garlic cloves, minced

3 cups [900 g] canned pumpkin

2 cups [480 ml] vegetable broth

2 cups [480 ml] full-fat coconut milk

2 Tbsp maple syrup

1 tsp kosher salt

½ tsp ground cinnamon

½ tsp curry powder

½ tsp garam masala

⅛ tsp cayenne pepper

Pepitas, for garnish

1 In a large heavy-bottomed pot, heat the olive oil over medium heat.

2 Turn the heat down to medium-low, then add the onions and garlic to the warm oil and sauté for 3 to 5 minutes, until the onions are translucent. Be careful not to brown the garlic.

3 Stir in the pumpkin, broth, coconut milk, maple syrup, salt, cinnamon, curry powder, garam masala, and cayenne. Turn the heat up to medium and let simmer for 20 minutes, stirring occasionally.

4 If desired, blitz the soup in a blender or with an immersion blender to get a silky-smooth consistency.

5 Top with a sprinkle of pepitas and serve hot.

Pumpkin Gnocchi with Cinnamon Sage Brown Butter Sauce

SERVES 4 | **PREP TIME** 20 MINUTES | **TOTAL TIME** 35 MINUTES

ONE OF THE FIRST THINGS I taught myself to make in college was gnocchi from scratch. I'm not sure why I decided to jump from packaged ramen to homemade "pasta"—and I say this lightly, because gnocchi technically isn't a pasta. It's a dumpling made from potatoes that happens to look identical to pasta. My gnocchi might have been misshapen, but it sure was delicious. And surprisingly, it didn't take that much time to create it from scratch.

This dish is a twist on the classic *gnocchi alla salvia* (gnocchi with sage), which calls for sage, butter, salt, and pepper. Sage and potato are a popular Italian pairing, and the two balance each other out perfectly. Just add in a bit of pumpkin, cinnamon, and other seasonal spices, and you've got the perfect "pasta" for fall.

INGREDIENTS

1 large russet potato
1½ cups [180 g] all-purpose flour, plus
   more for kneading
1 tsp kosher salt, plus more as needed
1 tsp pumpkin pie spice
1½ Tbsp light brown sugar
1 cup [300 g] pumpkin purée
4 Tbsp [55 g] unsalted butter
20 sage leaves
1 tsp ground cinnamon
2 Tbsp maple syrup
Freshly ground black pepper

1 Peel and cut the potato into quarters. Place the potato chunks in a medium pot and cover with about 2 in [5 cm] of water. Bring to a boil and cook for about 15 minutes, until the potato chunks are fork-tender. Drain and finely mash the potato. Set aside to cool.

2 In a small bowl, whisk together the flour, brown sugar, salt, and pie spice.

3 Lightly flour a clean work surface and tip out about ¾ cup [180 ml] of the mashed potato onto the floured surface. (If you have extra mashed potato, eat it as a snack!) Sift the flour mixture on top of the mashed potato, then scoop the pumpkin purée on top of the flour. With your hands, begin to gently knead the dough. Add an additional 1 Tbsp of flour at a time if the dough seems too wet. Knead until the dough is smooth.

4 Form the dough into a rectangular shape about ½ in [12 mm] thick. Using a knife, cut the dough horizontally into 1 in [2.5 cm] wide strips.

5 Take a strip and roll it into a rope about ½ in [12 mm] thick. Cut ½ in [12 mm] pieces off each rope to create gnocchi pieces. Place each piece on a tray in a single layer. Repeat with the remaining dough, flouring the surface lightly in between rolling each rope. Optional: Gently roll each piece of gnocchi over the back of a fork or a gnocchi board to create ridges in the dough.

6 Bring a large pot of salted water to a boil.

7 While waiting for the water to boil, prepare the butter sauce. In a medium-large pan over medium-high heat, melt the butter. Allow the butter to foam, add the sage, and then let the butter brown for 3 to 4 minutes. When the sage leaves begin to brown and crisp, remove them from the butter and discard. Turn the heat down to medium-low and

stir in the cinnamon and maple syrup. Be cautious; it will foam. Remove from the heat.

8 Once the water is boiling, drop in the gnocchi and stir to prevent them from clumping. Allow to cook for 3 minutes, or until the gnocchi begin to float. Once the gnocchi are finished cooking, drain and place directly into the saucepan with the sage butter sauce. Turn the heat to medium and sauté the gnocchi until they are golden and begin to crisp.

9 Plate and serve immediately with the sauce poured over the top. Season with salt and pepper, if desired.

FOOD

Pumpkin Spice Latte Trifle

SERVES 14 | **PREP TIME** 20 MINUTES | **TOTAL TIME** 1 HOUR

BELIEVE IT OR NOT, I never really grew up with pumpkin desserts. Instead of pumpkin pie, my family always served sweet potato pie at Thanksgiving—which I never complained about. It wasn't until I went off to college and attended a fall potluck dinner that I experienced the magic of pumpkin desserts.

This Pumpkin Spice Latte Trifle is a layered dessert of gingersnap/spice cookies, pumpkin mousse, and coffee-flavored custard. If you're an avid fan of a PSL, this dessert will be right up your alley. The coffee flavor balances out this sweet treat nicely, and it can double as a late-night snack or a morning delight.

FOOD

INGREDIENTS

2 cups [480 ml] heavy cream

One 8 oz [226 g] package cream cheese, at room temperature

¾ cup [150 g] sugar

One 15 oz [425 g] can pumpkin purée

One 3.4 oz [96 g] package instant vanilla pudding mix

1 tsp ground cinnamon

½ tsp ground ginger

⅛ tsp ground nutmeg

⅛ tsp ground clove

½ cup [120 ml] whole milk

¼ cup [22 g] instant espresso

¼ cup hot water

14 oz [395 g] gingersnap cookies, slightly crumbled

1 Using a hand or stand mixer, whip the cream until stiff peaks form. Scoop into a medium bowl, cover with a lid or plastic wrap, and refrigerate.

2 To create the pumpkin mousse, use a hand or stand mixer to whip the cream cheese and ½ cup [100 g] of the sugar until light and fluffy. Add the pumpkin, pudding mix, cinnamon, ginger, nutmeg, and clove. Once fully combined, slowly mix in the milk. Gently fold half of the whipped cream into the pumpkin batter. Be cautious not to overmix. Tip into a new bowl, cover, and refrigerate.

3 To create the espresso layer, use a hand or stand mixer to whip the instant espresso, remaining ¼ cup [50 g] of sugar, and hot water for approximately 5 minutes. The whipped coffee will be light in color and have a meringue-like consistency. Fold in the remaining whipped cream and be careful not to overmix. Set aside.

4 In a 3½ qt [3.3 L] trifle bowl or glass serving
dish, gently layer half of the crumbled cookies,
pumpkin mousse, and whipped coffee. Repeat
the layers, cover, and refrigerate for a minimum
of 40 minutes before serving.

November

NOVEMBER MAKES ME WANT TO REACH FOR MY STRETCHY PANTS, get cozy, spend a little more time in the kitchen, and enjoy evenings by the fire with friends and family. Of the three months in this book, November is when I most feel like I've made my house a home. You're piling on the layers, gearing up to transition to the holidays, and gathering with folks to eat copious amounts of food. What's not to love?

If November were a feeling, it would be the feeling of a giant hug. By this point, you have settled into the season, crossed off many things on your bucket list, and are enjoying the last bit of fall foliage and comfy nights at home before the craziness of the holidays begins. Savor all these moments—they always seem to go by way too fast.

The theme of this month is **gather**. With Thanksgiving and all the Friendsgiving celebrations happening, November is the perfect time to try new recipes packed with all of the best seasonal ingredients, experiment with some new-to-you wine varietals and cocktails, celebrate with friends, and be thankful with family.

And don't forget to soak up every last second of fall. The season might be drawing to a close, but there are still a few weeks left. I truly hope you have the best November full of family, friends, gratitude, and giving back.

November Gratitude Calendar

ACTIVITY

A LOT OF FOLKS CELEBRATE THE MONTH of December with an Advent calendar, which is always a good time. (Plus, if you have kids, they love it!) It's thrilling to open up a new window each day, knowing you're in for a surprise.

I truly believe that the thirty magical days of November deserve their own sort of specialty calendar as well. However, instead of celebrating the month with gifts or chocolate, why not give yourself the opportunity to practice gratitude each day?

Over the past few years, I've taken a step back and tried to focus more on the good, rather than any bad things or minor inconveniences that get me down. It's not always easy to stay in a positive mindset, but when you practice gratitude, it can really put everything into perspective and help you stay calm, cool, and collected throughout the day.

I suggest keeping a gratitude journal year-round. Take the time each morning or evening to jot down what you're grateful for in a blank journal, or purchase a gratitude journal and follow the prompts. If you don't already have a gratitude journal, try keeping one this month for 30 days and see how much this habit changes your outlook on life.

Alternatively, create a gratitude calendar with daily prompts that your entire household can enjoy. While you might not receive a gift each day, what you'll gain in the long run will be so much better than a material item. For a fun twist, write what you're grateful for on faux leaves and place them in a bowl. At the end of the month, draw some leaves from the bowl at the dinner table, and share what you're grateful for with your household, family, or friends who are participating in this tradition!

Here are some sample gratitude prompts for your November Gratitude Calendar, or feel free to come up with your own! →

30 Days of Gratefulness

1 What's a hobby that refreshes you?

2 Tell your family why you're thankful for them.

3 What friend are you thankful for?

4 What is a place that you're thankful for?

5 What food are you the most thankful for?

6 Who is a teacher that had a positive impact on your life growing up?

7 What do you love about your hometown?

8 What song or album are you grateful for?

9 What's a small gesture that a friend, partner, or family member did recently that made your day?

10 In what way is nature beautiful to you?

11 What is one of your favorite memories?

12 What's a future event that you're excited about?

13 Name something positive about your body.

14 What's one good thing that happened today?

15 What kindness did someone give to you today?

16 What do you like about the current season?

17 What's the most thoughtful gift you've ever received?

18 What's a personality trait that you're grateful for?

19 What freedoms are you grateful for?

20 What is your favorite family tradition?

21 What's a challenge that you're grateful for?

22 What do you like the most about your job or school?

23 Who has helped you during a trying time?

24 Name one public figure who's had a big impact on your life.

25 What's your favorite part of the morning?

26 What's something that made you laugh today?

27 Name a smell that you love.

28 Name three accomplishments that you're proud of.

29 What's something that you're passionate about?

30 What's a technology that you're thankful for?

ACTIVITY

SELF-CARE: HOW TO BOUNCE BACK

After Daylight Saving Ends

EITHER YOU LOVE OR HATE DAYLIGHT SAVING TIME. I'm a big fan of it when there's still daylight at 9:00 p.m. in the summer, but in the fall when it gets dark before dinnertime? It's not as appealing!

That Monday after daylight saving time ends is pretty much the worst. You feel disoriented and groggy, your sleep schedule is out of whack, and if you have pets, there's a good chance that they won't understand the time shift either and beg for food at the incorrect time. Plus, it's been scientifically proven that DST messes up our internal clock.

So, how do you gracefully adjust to life after daylight saving time? Here are a few tips to make that transition seamless. (You can also apply these same tips if you're traveling—they'll help you beat jet lag as well.)

- **AVOID COFFEE AND ALCOHOL:** Try to stop drinking coffee 4 to 6 hours before bedtime, because it can interfere with your sleep schedule. Yes to the morning coffee, but try to skip that afternoon espresso. Alcohol can also affect your sleep schedule and prohibit you from getting quality sleep, so skip the booze that first week while you're getting adjusted to the time shift.

- **TRY TO FORGO NAPS:** Your first instinct might be to take naps to get some energy back during the day. A power nap of 20 minutes is perfectly acceptable—it's enough to give you an energy boost without throwing off your internal clock. However, anything longer than that will make it harder for you to get a full night of quality sleep. Best to just power through the day and hit the sack at a reasonable hour.

- **BE CONSISTENT WITH YOUR SCHEDULE:** Don't shift your schedule an hour back or forward to compensate for the time difference. If you had a specific routine, stick to it as closely as possible. Additionally, try to avoid hitting snooze on your alarm each morning. When you stick to your schedule, it will make it easier to transition to the new season. Plus, if you wake up early enough to catch the sunlight, it will invigorate you and help jump-start your day.

- **PRACTICE GOOD HABITS BEFORE BEDTIME:** This is something that can and should be done 24/7/365. Look at your bedtime routine and see if there's room for improvement. If you're watching TV, scrolling through your phone, or on your computer right before bed, you'll want to nip that in the bud. Avoid all electronics an hour before bedtime. The blue light that these electronics emit stimulates your brain the same way the sun does and makes it harder for you to get to sleep at a reasonable time. Try reading a book or doing a skin-care routine during that time before bed instead. For optimal quality of sleep, also avoid working out in the 4 to 6 hours before bedtime.

- **IMPLEMENT A "LIGHT SCHEDULE":** The most important thing to do when daylight saving time ends is expose yourself to as much sunlight as possible to keep your internal clock running. If you're waking up before sunrise, you can purchase a lamp that mimics natural sunlight to get your body on the right schedule. Also, go for short walks when it's light outside. If you're not exposed to enough light, it can affect your serotonin levels. Make sure you're getting as much sunlight as possible, real or fake, during this shift.

HOST A
Beer or Cider Tasting

THE WORLD OF CRAFT BEER can be a bit overwhelming to a newbie. In addition to the beers you see from bigger distributors at your local grocery store, there are thousands of craft breweries worldwide, which produce a variety of beers ranging from light to dark. So, how do you figure out which beer you enjoy out of the thousands of options available? You go beer tasting, of course!

Hosting a beer tasting can be a fun way to experience and introduce new beers and new styles of beer to you and your friends. This is a great year-round activity, but I love beer tasting in the fall so I can try all the seasonal offerings available. Hello, pumpkin lager!

If you want to host a beer tasting at home, be sure to keep these tips in mind.

Have Enough of the Same Glassware for All Your Guests

Different glasses can affect the taste of beer. Get everyone on the same page by having the same type of glass for everyone tasting.

The most traditional glass for beer is the pint glass. It's a versatile glass that complements most kinds of beer, from IPAs to stouts, ales, and lagers. If you want to get a sense of the aromatics of the beer, snifter glasses are ideal. Beer is easy to swirl in these glasses—but make sure you don't fill them all the way to the top. Pilsner glasses work well for both pilsners and lighter beers. A stemmed tulip glass is great for saisons, Belgian beers, and ales. Lastly, a goblet is one of the most extravagant glasses to drink beer with, and if you're looking for an elevated way to taste beer, this would be a solid bet.

Keep Beer Sealed and in the Fridge as Long as Possible

The taste of beer can change drastically as it gets warmer, so be sure to serve beer at its coldest and best temperature.

Snacks Are Key

Having snacks while tasting helps you figure out what the beer will taste like when paired with food. Plus, it'll keep you from tasting on an empty stomach.

Serve plenty of finger foods and bite-size snacks at your beer tasting. Cheese, sausages, pretzels, french fries, salted nuts, and chips and dips are perfect snacks to pair with beer.

Get More Beers Than You Think You'll Need

And make sure they're all chilled. Someone will always want to try a bit more or have a favorite that they'll want to revisit after the tasting.

Create a Theme

All of the options of craft beer can be overwhelming, so why not narrow them down to one style or region to make it easier for your guests to remember? You can pick a country (Belgium, Ireland) or a region (North Carolina, New England), try a variety of pumpkin beers, or even sample beers from the same brand.

Beer Styles to Look For

- **IPAS:** India pale ale, or IPA, is a very broad category of beer. From fruity to bitter, these hop-forward ales encompass a vast majority of craft brewing today.

- **LAGERS:** A lager was most likely the first style of beer that you tried because they're easy drinking crowd-pleasers. Pick up some lagers from your local breweries to taste all the range this style can offer.

- **SOURS:** This style of beer is intentionally acidic or tart. Some sour beers are cellared and aged like wine!

- **STOUTS:** Stouts are dark beers with many different variations. These beers offer some of the most diverse flavors of all. Try stouts that have fruit additions or oatmeal, or that are barrel-aged.

Must-Have Outerwear

FOR COLDER DAYS

AS THE TEMPERATURES COOL DOWN, one thing is for certain: Layering is going to be your best friend.

Whether you live in a mild climate or somewhere that gets very hot summers and freezing winters, having these five types of outerwear will ensure you're prepared for any type of weather.

- **THE CASUAL, LIGHTWEIGHT JACKET:** This is your laid-back, "I just came here to run a few errands" jacket. You put this jacket on with a T-shirt and jeans and boom—you instantly look put together. Everyone needs a worry-free, casual jacket.

  I'm a big fan of an olive-green utility jacket. It works year-round, goes with pretty much everything, and is a timeless layering option. However, lightweight trench coats, blazers, and sweater coats are also solid bets.

- **THE DENIM JACKET:** A denim jacket is one of the go-to types of outerwear in my closet. A classic denim jacket will never go out of style, but you can always play with different silhouettes to update the trend. I love to layer a denim jacket over skirts and dresses to dress a look down, or pair it with leggings, a tee, and some sneakers for a laid-back yet put-together ensemble. If you're bold enough, you can even attempt a denim-on-denim look!

- **THE (FAUX) LEATHER JACKET:** This is a piece you'll reach for every time fall comes around. A leather jacket is a super-versatile item that you can wear on date night, while running errands, to work . . . the list goes on!

  A leather jacket is a bit heavier than a denim jacket, so it's great for those evenings that are unexpectedly chilly. I recommend sizing up if purchasing a leather jacket, just in case you need to layer a sweater or a sweatshirt underneath.

A classic black leather jacket will always be in style, or pick a leather jacket in a different color, like brown or burgundy, or one with embellishments to add some flair.

- **THE STATEMENT COAT:** Headed to a wedding? A fancy night out? An elegant Thanksgiving? Feel like dressing up just because? You might want to invest in a statement coat that you can wear for dressier occasions.

A cozy leopard coat never goes out of style. Or play with different fabrics, textures, and bold colors to find the best statement coat for you. If the coat doesn't make you feel chic as all get out, it's not worth it.

- **THE WARM WINTER COAT:** This is probably the most obvious type of coat that you need, but go ahead and get yourself a nice, warm winter coat. Keyword: warm.

Choose a coat that hits your knee (or longer!), so you can stay cozy no matter what the temperature is. Look for either wool coats or down coats; these will keep you toasty even on the chilliest fall nights, so that you can comfortably enjoy all your favorite fall activities.

Pro tip: You can always add a jacket liner underneath if your coat isn't quite warm enough.

Transitioning Your Skin-Care Routine

TO COLDER MONTHS

IT'S A GOOD IDEA TO SWITCH UP your skin-care routine this time of year. Depending on where you live, with the cooler air of the season also comes a drop in humidity, and dry air can cause dry skin. The uptick in indoor heating and inclement weather can also draw out moisture and leave you with drier skin as well. Dry skin can lead to itchy skin, which can wreak all sorts of havoc. Here are a few things you can do to transition your skin-care routine in the fall, regardless of your skin type.

- **INCREASE THE THICKNESS OF YOUR MOISTURIZER:** Use a lighter moisturizer in the spring and summer, and stick to a thicker moisturizer in the colder months. Look for thicker moisturizers that work with your skin type: dry, combination, or oily skin, or if you're acne prone. There is no one-size-fits-all when it comes to moisturizers, but

you'll definitely want to opt for more moisture during the fall and winter.

- **USE A HUMIDIFIER AT NIGHT:** Even if you're using a thicker moisturizer, the dry air can still strip your skin of moisture. When you're using heat or forced air in your home during colder months, it can reduce the humidity to as low as 10 percent. A humidifier is great for a couple of reasons: In addition to providing much needed moisture in the air of a room, it can also relieve symptoms of colds and sinus infections. Win-win! Opt for a whole-house humidifier system, or a single unit humidifier to keep in the bedroom. If you travel frequently, look into a portable humidifier that you can take with you in order to keep your skin in the best shape wherever you go.

- **KEEP USING SUNSCREEN:** UVB rays might not be as strong in autumn, but UVA rays (a.k.a. the ones that cause skin cancer and premature wrinkles) are just as strong as they are in July and August. You might be exposed to less sunlight in the fall, but it's still important to wear SPF daily.

- **ADD IN HYDRATING MASKS:** A thicker moisturizer might not be enough to prevent dry skin, so consider applying a super hydrating mask one or two times a week to keep your skin as moisturized as possible. As always, find a mask that is ideal for your skin type and skin-care concerns.

- **STAY HYDRATED:** Hydration is important year-round, but especially so in the fall. The more hydrated you are on the inside, the better your skin will look on the outside. I like to drink a glass of hot water with lemon every single morning before I have my coffee (or anything else). The hot beverage will leave you feeling cozy, and it's a great way to get a jump-start on hydration for the day. If you're on the go, carry a reusable water bottle with you to have easy access to water all day long.

FIVE WAYS TO
Give Back

ACTIVITY

ONE REASON I LOVE THE MONTH OF NOVEM-BER is that it's a time to gather with friends, reflect, and be thankful for what you have.

Even though there's a lot going on in November, from Friendsgivings to Thanksgivings to holiday prep, it's important to slow down, practice gratitude, and give back if you're able to. If you're thankful for what you have and are in a position to help others, I would highly encourage you to do so.

The best part? You don't always have to make a monetary donation to give back. Volunteering your time or making use of your skills are also great ways to give to your community!

Gather In-Kind Donations for Charity

One way to give to a charity? Find out what items they're looking for and see if you have anything around the house that might fit the bill. Animal shelters typically have wish lists that include pet food, toys, and harnesses; homeless shelters usually need books, new linens, and toiletries; and food banks are always in need of nonperishable goods.

Instead of donating these items on your own, why not encourage some friends, coworkers, or neighbors to join you? Share with your circles that you're making a donation to a group in need, and offer to drop off donations for others. You'd be surprised at how much you can collectively give to an organization doing important work in the community!

Feed the Hungry

With all the food you'll be enjoying with friends and family this season, why not give food to those in need?

A few ways that you can feed the hungry this holiday season are by filling your community fridge, organizing a pop-up free grocery store, or feeding your neighbors or church family members. Or pack extra lunches and keep them with you in case you run into someone who is in need while you're out and about.

Want to go above and beyond? Contact your local food bank or food pantry to learn other ways you can be of assistance.

Use Your Voice and Encourage Others

I think that pretty much everyone on social media has influence, whether they're deemed an "influencer" or not. Think about it: that restaurant you posted about and your friends went to? The hairstylist you highly recommended that your parent ended up booking an appointment with? We're all influencers in some way, shape, or form—don't underestimate your ability to influence people to do the right thing!

I love that social media has made it super easy to organize fundraisers, inspire donations, and be vocal about important issues. Use your platform to encourage friends and family to give this season!

Pay It Forward

This is something so small and simple that can really make someone's day. I still remember the day I was in a drive-thru line to grab coffee, and the cashier informed me that the car in front of mine had paid for my order. I never forgot how surprised and delighted I was in that moment—so much so, that I decided to pay for the car behind mine's order.

Any way you choose to pay it forward—footing the bill for food, groceries, or toys—can really brighten someone's day. You can also offer to pay utility bills for seniors, leave a gift card at a gas pump, or tuck a grocery store gift card in a shopping basket for the next shopper to stumble upon!

Volunteer Virtually

You don't have to leave the comfort of your own home to volunteer. When volunteering virtually, you can pick either short-term tasks or long-term projects, both of which can be completed off-site. If you have a smartphone or access to a computer, you can find so many ways to volunteer from home.

Some ways that you can volunteer virtually include advocating for causes, transcribing or translating materials, helping organize campaigns, and more.

ACTIVITY

WATCH IT!

The Best Thanksgiving TV Episodes

ACTIVITY

ARE YOUR THANKSGIVINGS FULL OF LAUGHTER or a bit dramatic? Gathering around the table with friends and family can either be an absolute hoot or a total disaster. Regardless of the outcome, one thing's for sure: Thanksgiving makes for pretty awesome television.

Grab a blanket and a warm drink, cozy up on the couch, and binge-watch some of these iconic Thanksgiving TV episodes on your streaming service of choice. ➤

Top Seven Classic Thanksgiving TV Episodes

- **MASTER OF NONE (SEASON 2, EPISODE 8)** – This critically acclaimed episode written by Lena Waithe explores the challenges of coming out to her family during a series of Thanksgivings from the 1990s to the present. You'll want to grab tissues for this episode—throughout, you see Denise accept her sexuality and become more comfortable with her true self.

- **BLACK-ISH (SEASON 3, EPISODE 7)** – If you need a good laugh, this episode of *Black-ish* is right up your alley. In this Thanksgiving special, Pops's older sister unexpectedly arrives for Thanksgiving, and the children try to figure out the mystery behind their great-aunt.

- **THE MINDY PROJECT (SEASON 1, EPISODE 6)** – This episode is hilarious, a bit awkward, and incredibly relatable. The title character of the show, Mindy, has an unexpected run-in with a former blind date and his new girlfriend—and the end result is incredibly entertaining.

- **NEW GIRL (SEASON 1, EPISODE 6)** – The casting on *New Girl* is perfect, and every time I watch these roommates' shenanigans, I end up crying laughing. In this episode, Jess invites a music teacher from her school that she's always had a crush on to her roommate's big Thanksgiving dinner—and naturally, things spin out of control quickly.

- **GOSSIP GIRL (SEASON 1, EPISODE 9)** – This is one of the best episodes of *Gossip Girl* of all time. Drama runs rampant when Dan's and Serena's parents are put in an awkward situation and their families unexpectedly spend Thanksgiving together. Plus, Nate and Blair find themselves in uncomfortable situations as well. This episode is chaotic in the best way possible.

- **GILMORE GIRLS (SEASON 3, EPISODE 9)** – This episode is a spectacular piece of television. The writing is incredible! Watch Lorelai and Rory go to four Thanksgiving dinners in a single day, and during one, Rory shares a surprise with Lorelai that she struggles to process.

- **THE WEST WING (SEASON 2, EPISODE 8)** – If you like your Thanksgiving with a side of chaos, this episode of *The West Wing* is perfect for you. There's a glimpse of Thanksgiving at the White House, along with a political crisis and a boy picking fights in school.

Thanksgiving Crafts

(WITH OR WITHOUT KIDS)

PERSONALIZE YOUR HOME THIS NOVEMBER and add festive touches with some of these simple Thanksgiving crafts. All these are easy, unexpected, and fun to do with or without children.

Make Place Cards with Mini Pumpkins

This project will take only minutes to complete, but will make a huge impact on your tablescape. You'll need mini pumpkins, an X-Acto knife, patterned scrapbook paper, cardstock in a coordinating solid color, glue, and a marker. Carefully make a slit at the top of your pumpkin to insert the place card. (You could also use pomegranates or persimmons here.) Cut leaf shapes out of the patterned paper, and rectangles out of the solid cardstock. Glue the patterned leaves onto the cardstock and let dry. Write your guest's name on top, perhaps in a gold metallic marker. After you're done creating the place cards, slot them into your pumpkin place card holders.

Bedazzle Gourds

Anyone else out there love their bedazzler growing up? This DIY will give you the most decadent gourds on your block, and is a less-messy alternative to carving pumpkins. Just take a couple packs of rhinestones, remove the sticker backing, and apply them— simple as that! Try a stripe pattern with alternating columns of rhinestones. Or, if you're feeling artistic, draw a pattern or shape (such as a monogram or a star) on your pumpkin with a pencil and use a hot glue gun to trace the outline of your shape. Then add rhinestones or flat-sided beads to the glue until your shape is complete.

Paint Rocks to Make a Centerpiece

Collect rocks that you find outside. (Don't take any rocks from public places, though! If they're not from your own yard, leave them be and instead, just order some rocks online.) Clean your rocks with soap and water to get any dust and debris off. Consider

spray-painting the rock as a base to make it even. Use acrylic paints and fall-themed stencils (both available at your local craft store) to paint your rocks. Or freehand paint! Mix up the designs and add them to your Thanksgiving tablescape for a one-of-a-kind look.

Make Your Own Felt Coasters

For this, get synthetic felt in an array of fall colors that are 12 by 8 in [30.5 by 20 cm] with $\frac{1}{16}$ in [2 mm] thickness—think rust, burgundy, brown, and yellow. Find a 4 in [10 cm] hexagon template and a small leaf template online. Cut out felt hexagon shapes and small leaves using your templates. Using a quick-dry all-purpose adhesive, apply the leaves on top of the hexagon cutouts and press with heavy books for at least 10 minutes. This is a great craft to do with family each Thanksgiving, and you can enjoy the fruits of your labor at the dinner table all fall long.

Games for Friendsgiving

ONE OF THE MAIN REASONS I LOVE FRIENDS-GIVING is that it's oftentimes way more laid back and casual than Thanksgiving with the extended family. You can gather with peers that are the same age as you, have a few drinks (or mocktails!), and let the good times roll.

Friendsgiving is a time to get together with your favorite friends, celebrate your friend-ship, and naturally, get so competitive while playing games that said friendships are irrep-arably broken. I kid, I kid, but here are four great game ideas for your next Friendsgiving.

- **CHARADES:** Charades is a classic game and super easy to organize with limited sup-plies. Form two teams. Have everyone write down names of celebrities, random objects, events, or titles of movies, books, plays—whatever springs to mind!—on strips of paper. Fold all the strips and place them in a bowl. Taking turns, a representative from each team picks a clue and gets 45 seconds to act it out for their team to guess. No talking, sounds, or noises allowed! If the team guesses it right, the representative can pick another clue and keep going until their time is up. Each correct guess is one point.

- **PICTIONARY:** Pictionary is a spin on cha-rades, but instead of acting out the clues, the representative has to draw them!

- **CAMOUFLAGE:** For this game, you'll need to collect fifteen to twenty small house-hold items, such as a paper clip, pen, stamp, quarter, rubber band, or stick of gum. Type up a list of the items and print out as many copies as you have guests. The organizer should then hide all the items in plain sight in a single room or area of the house. (For example, adhere a postage stamp to the spine of a book on a bookshelf; lay a pen across the top of a picture frame; put things high up or down low, inside a lampshade or in a flower arrangement. Items should be hard to find but still visible.) You can play this in pairs or small teams, or every person for themselves. Players then get a certain amount of time,

say 10 minutes, to browse through the room looking for the items (without touching anything) and recording the hiding spots on their personal list. Make sure guests don't reveal the hiding spots by reacting when they see an item! Everyone will be searching at the same time, so they should be stealthy about it. At the end of the time limit, or once someone finds all the items on the list, whoever finds the most items wins.

- **THE NEWLYWED GAME:** Is your Friendsgiving full of couples? Play the newlywed game, and find out which pair knows the most about the other. This is a simple game where a host asks one half of a couple a question about themselves and the other half has to guess what their answer is. Points are awarded when both members' answers match, and it is always a hoot. You think you know your partner, but in reality, they might end up surprising you!

A Thanksgiving Tablescape

WHEN I HOSTED MY FIRST THANKSGIVING YEARS AGO, it was invigorating. I had attended Thanksgiving at friends' and family's houses for years, and when it was my turn, I experienced the most incredible joy planning my ideal menu and designing my own space for the beloved festivities.

Nowadays, when I host Thanksgiving, I look forward to planning the tablescape the most. This is something you can plan several weeks in advance, and you can set up your tablescape a couple of weeks before Thanksgiving or Friendsgiving to stay in the festive spirit at home.

Designing a Thanksgiving tablescape can seem like a daunting task. Most of us aren't interior designers, and we are working with limited budgets. However, creating a beautiful tablescape doesn't have to be difficult or expensive. Here are some tips and tricks to help you nail the perfect table!

Curate a Color Scheme

First things first: What color scheme are you feeling? You could opt for a traditional color range of oranges, reds, browns, and yellows, or you could mix things up and create a color scheme that suits your style and decor. Some of my favorite unexpected color combinations for Thanksgiving are orange and white; pale green and gold; pink and gray; and cream and aubergine.

Thrift or Rent Products to Save Money

Let's face it: You'll likely only use a good chunk of the items from this tablescape a handful of times each year. As tempting as it is to buy all brand-new items for your tablescape, why not rent or thrift items to save a bit of money?

To rent, look up local party rental stores to see if they have chargers, china, table runners, or other seasonal props for rent. You can also find some incredible party rental shops online—places like Social Studies, Hestia Harlow, and Freshly Set have stylish tablescape rental options.

Start with a Table Runner or Tablecloth

To kick off your tablescape design, start by picking a table runner or a tablecloth. I love table runners on a nice wooden or textured table; otherwise, consider a tablecloth. Whether you go for a colorful fabric or keep things neutral, this is a great place to figure out what accents will work, too. For example, if you have a warm-hued tablecloth, such as marigold or rust, go for gold or copper flatware, candles, and decor. If your color scheme is cooler, either silver or gold accents can work.

Skip the Huge Centerpiece

While it's tempting to go big or go home with the centerpiece during Thanksgiving, the larger your centerpiece is, the harder it can be for your guests to have a conversation across the table. Instead of choosing one large centerpiece, why not opt for a centerpiece that's shorter in height? You can still add some tall, thin taper candles to create height and dimension, but you'll also enjoy an uninterrupted view.

Pile on the Pumpkins, Gourds, and Greenery

I love to use a mix of real and faux mini pumpkins and gourds for a Thanksgiving tablescape. Select a range of sizes and colors, such as white and orange, or pastel pink and pale green. Amass them in the center of your table on top of your runner for an abundant look, or intermingle them among bud vases with single bloom flowers.

Depending on the vibe, consider adding in some greenery. A simple eucalyptus garland is always a solid bet, and you can easily augment it with some late season dahlias, roses, sprigs of herbs, winter artichokes, or protea. Other greenery that works nicely as a garland includes olive leaves, magnolia leaves, boxwood, and fir.

DECOR & DIY

Make It Cozy with Candles

When it comes to decor, the more candlelight, the better. I love adding candles for special occasions, because they remind me of some of the nicest meals out at restaurants. Try an assortment of votive candles in different sizes, or use a collection of tall taper candles and elegant candlesticks.

For an easy alternative to a garland or floral centerpiece, make a "runner" out of candles. Group as many of the same or similar candles as you can fit down the center of your table— simple glass votives in varying sizes, an assortment of gold mercury glass votives, or votives of the same size in a cohesive, autumnal color scheme, such as Glassybaby candles, would all work well for this.

Match the Plates
and Flatware to the Menu

In general, you should have a dinner plate, salad plate, and either a charger or a place mat for each table setting. Unless you're having a soup course, you likely won't need bowls, but double-check the menu and see if it's something you'll need. Remember the dessert plates or bowls too, if you're serving pie or ice cream.

Also, make sure you have the right amount of flatware for your menu! Don't forget flatware for each course, butter spreaders and steak knives, dessert forks and spoons, and coffee spoons if you need them.

DIY Some Decor

Spray-paint mini pumpkins to match your color scheme and write your guests' names on them in a metallic pen or permanent marker. DIY place cards! You could also use persimmons or pomegranates as place card holders (see page 130). Even simple paper place cards make an event feel more glamorous and professional. These kinds of DIY projects are inexpensive and add a fantastic, personalized touch!

DECOR & DIY

THE ULTIMATE
Thanksgiving Cheese Board

HAVE YOU EVER GONE TO A WINERY OR A CHEESE SHOP and wondered how on earth they make their cheese boards look so incredible?

Trust me: Once you get the hang of it, it's not that hard to craft the perfect cheese board at home.

I love a good cheese board for Thanksgiving because it gives your guests something to graze on while the turkey is in the oven and their stomachs are grumbling in anticipation of the beloved, seasonal feast. And let's face it: Those pre-Thanksgiving snacks are the only thing keeping us from becoming completely hangry and miserable before dinner is served.

If you want to satiate your guests' hunger and dazzle them with your host(ess) skills, you can create your own Instagram-worthy cheese spread for your next Friendsgiving or Thanksgiving. Here's how to craft the perfect seasonal board in four easy steps.

Select the Cheese(s)

To start, pick three to five different kinds of cheese for your board, depending on how many guests are in attendance. If you have five guests or fewer, three cheeses are a good amount. Ten or more guests? Go with five cheeses. If you want to get fancy with it, you can stick to a particular region—French cheeses always seem to be a hit, or you could opt for Italian or Spanish cheeses. Always select at least one soft cheese and one hard cheese for your board to accommodate your guests' preferences.

The board pictured on pages 138 to 139 features a few of my go-to French cheeses: a type of triple crème, Camembert, and Comté. If you have the time and *really* want to be a show-off, carve a leaf shape into one of your round, soft cheeses, and place pomegranate seeds in the cutout. Will it be extra? Yes. Will your guests love it? Absolutely.

Place the cheeses on your board first, spacing them out so there's plenty of room between them, and add all the extras afterward.

Add Fruit and Nut Accompaniments

Next up, it's time to add a few more bells and whistles to this board. Choose fruit and nut options that will pair well with the cheeses you've selected. (You can always ask your local cheesemonger for recommendations if you're not sure!) Make sure to have some ramekins on hand for your desired dips and condiments.

Some of my favorite fruit and accompaniment options for Thanksgiving include:

- Honey or honeycomb
- Red or green grapes
- Sliced pears
- Blackberries
- Mixed olives or Castelvetrano olives
- Dijon mustard
- Cornichons
- Mango or peach chutney, fig jam, or quince paste
- Marcona almonds or candied pecans, depending on whether you prefer sweet or savory

Add Crackers and Bread

This step is the easiest: Stack and pile crackers and bread in the remaining open spaces of your board to ensure it feels really full and abundant. Rosemary raisin crisps will give you a delicious burst of fall flavor. Assorted entertainment crackers, breadsticks, toasted baguette slices, or torn focaccia pieces would all be great additions as well.

Add Some Garnishes

Take your Thanksgiving board to the next level and include some garnishes to make it extra special. Add some seasonal decor like mini pumpkins and gourds; herbs and greens such as rosemary, thyme, or dill will look and smell fresh; or try adding some cranberries for a pop of color to make it look even more festive.

The Best Wines

FOR THANKSGIVING (OR FRIENDSGIVING)

WHETHER YOU'RE ATTENDING A FRIENDSGIVING or hosting your family for Turkey Day, one thing's for sure: You're going to want a delicious wine to accompany your spread. The perfect wine has the potential to elevate your meal and bring out unexpected flavors in your food.

Ideally if you're hosting, have a few wine options for your guests: Aim for three or four different varietals (red, white, bubbly), just to cover your bases. If you're a guest, it's polite to bring a bottle (or two!), especially if you're picky when it comes to your vino.

So, which wines will pair well with your meal? Here's a cheat sheet to help you find the best wines for Thanksgiving dinner!

The Perfect Whites

- **CHENIN BLANC:** It's not always easy to pair a wine with several dishes at Thanksgiving; however, Chenin Blanc is always a solid bet. South African Chenin Blancs have been growing in popularity in recent years (and are very underrated in my opinion). You can easily find a bottle for less than the cost of a

meal out, and they have a bold flavor profile that will pair perfectly with rich dishes without overpowering your sides.

- **RIESLING:** This white wine is fruity and flavorful but not too alcoholic. It is a fantastic option to pair with dishes that are spicy, salty, or sweet. You can opt for Rieslings that are either bone dry or semi-sweet: There's truly a Riesling that will work for every kind of palate!

- **VIOGNIER:** This is one of the most versatile wines for the holiday season! It's floral and fruity and a great complement to turkey.

The Perfect Reds

- **BEAUJOLAIS:** If you're going to serve any one red wine during Thanksgiving, a Beaujolais is the ideal choice. This is a light-bodied, low-tannin wine that is not too bold and will pair perfectly with all your Thanksgiving dishes. It is no-fuss and ready to drink now—no need to worry about aging it or putting it in a decanter for hours on end. You can serve your Beaujolais lightly chilled if you'd like!

- **ZINFANDEL:** A Zinfandel is more full-bodied and will give you a bit of spice during Thanksgiving dinner. It will uplift all your side dishes (e.g., potatoes, stuffing, etc.) without being overpowering. A California Zin from your local grocery store would be a safe bet!

- **PINOT NOIR:** This is probably the most classic Thanksgiving wine pairing, and for good reason: It has low tannins and can be light- to medium-bodied, and it's super versatile with food pairings.

- **SYRAH/SHIRAZ:** The peppery flavor of Syrah will pair incredibly well with your Thanksgiving dishes. Cool-climate Syrahs are a particularly great match for turkey and stuffing.

Sparkling and Dessert Wines

- **PROSECCO, CAVA, OR A SPARKLING ROSÉ:** Don't sleep on a sparkling wine pairing at Thanksgiving. It's festive and works nicely either as an aperitif or with apps before dinner. Plus, the acidity of a bubbly wine is great for either salty or fried foods. It could be the ideal wine for your meal from start to finish.

- **PORT OR SHERRY:** If you want a dessert wine, I'd highly recommend a good port or a sherry. A tawny port tastes a bit nuttier than a ruby port and is the perfect pairing for pie. Just be careful: Ports often have a higher alcohol content than regular wine, so don't go overboard while pouring them! A cream sherry will also pair nicely with any of the desserts you have on the table.

Cranberry Ginger Mocktail

SERVES 4 | **PREP TIME** 15 MINUTES | **TOTAL TIME** 20 MINUTES

DRINK

ONE THING THAT I LOVE TO SERVE DURING THANKSGIVING? A mocktail. Not everyone drinks alcoholic beverages, and I don't think those guests should feel left out during the festivities just because that isn't their thing. Don't serve them the store-bought iced tea: Handcraft a delicious mocktail that everyone can enjoy!

Cranberry is one of my favorite ingredients for fall food and cocktails. Cranberries are typically harvested between September and November in North America, so don't pass up the opportunity to use this seasonal fruit. A warm spice like ginger paired with sweet cranberry juice tastes like perfection.

This Cranberry Ginger Mocktail is light, refreshing, and something you'll reach for time and time again. Plus, it's a photo-worthy mocktail that your guests will adore, and something you can serve well into the holiday season.

INGREDIENTS

1 cup [200 g] sugar
1 cup [115 g] peeled and sliced fresh
   ginger root
½ vanilla bean
4 oz [120 ml] unsweetened cranberry
   juice
8 oz [240 ml] club soda

NOTE: *The ginger syrup can be made ahead and stored in the refrigerator for up to 2 weeks. Also, the drink base can be doubled in a large pitcher, and each individual drink can be topped off with fresh club soda.*

1 Combine the sugar, ginger, and vanilla bean with ¾ cup [180 ml] of water in a medium pot. Bring to a boil, then turn the heat to low and simmer for 10 minutes. Let cool to room temperature and strain.

2 To make the mocktails, place ice in four rocks glasses. Set aside.

3 In a large cocktail shaker, add 6 oz [180 ml] of the ginger syrup, the cranberry juice, and a handful of ice. Cover and shake for about 20 seconds. Strain equally into the four rocks glasses. Top each glass with 2 oz [60 ml] of fresh club soda.

Pear, Ginger, Star Anise Shrub

MAKES 3 CUPS [720 ML] | **PREP TIME** 5 MINUTES | **TOTAL TIME** 1.5 HOURS

PEARS ARE THE PERFECT FRUIT FOR FALL: Not only are they in season, but they're also juicy and crisp, and pair well with other quintessential fall produce. If you're making a homemade shrub, pear is an absolute must. Here's an easy pear and ginger shrub that you can make at home. Mix it with club soda, seltzer, or tonic for a mocktail, or shake it up with your preferred spirit.

DRINK

INGREDIENTS
1 cup [200 g] sugar
3 large ripe pears, unpeeled and sliced
1 in [2.5 cm] piece of fresh ginger,
   unpeeled and sliced
4 star anise pods
1 cup [240 ml] apple cider vinegar

1 In a medium-large pot with a lid, combine the sugar, pears, ginger, and star anise with 1 cup [240 ml] of water. Bring to a boil, then simmer over medium-low heat for 1 hour with the lid on, stirring occasionally.

2 Remove from the heat and stir in the apple cider vinegar. Allow the mixture to cool completely. Strain into a glass vessel with a lid. Store in the refrigerator for up to 3 weeks.

Cider Maple Old-Fashioned

SERVES 4 | **PREP TIME** 5 MINUTES | **TOTAL TIME** 5 MINUTES

ONE OF MY FAVORITE THINGS ABOUT AN OLD-FASHIONED is that it's fairly easy to tweak the recipe and make it more seasonally appropriate.

For this recipe, we're updating the classic old-fashioned with two seasonal ingredients that pair perfectly together: maple syrup and apple cider. The peppery flavor of the cider is a fantastic complement to the sweet syrup. As a general rule of thumb, the darker your maple syrup is, the more pronounced its flavor, so keep this in mind while selecting your ingredients for this magical seasonal cocktail.

DRINK

INGREDIENTS

1 cup [240 ml] apple cider

2 Tbsp maple syrup

6 dashes Angostura bitters

8 oz [240 ml] bourbon

4 cinnamon sticks, for garnish

4 orange twists, for garnish

1 In a large cocktail shaker, combine the apple cider, maple syrup, and bitters. Using a barspoon, give the mixture a good stir. Add the bourbon and four or five ice cubes. Stir until chilled, about 30 seconds.

2 Divide equally among four glasses. Garnish each with a cinnamon stick and an orange twist.

Maple Roasted Acorn Squash

SERVES 4 | **PREP TIME** 15 MINUTES | **TOTAL TIME** 45 MINUTES

LOOKING FOR THE PERFECT SIDE DISH FOR FALL? Well, my friend: Look no further.

Maple Roasted Acorn Squash is an easy-to-make side that screams fall. It's a little sweet, a little savory, and 100 percent delicious. I love that there's very little prep work involved with creating this dish, which makes it perfect for a casual dinner at home. My one recommendation? Use your favorite olive oil to really bring out the fall flavor in this dish!

INGREDIENTS

2 medium acorn squashes
3 Tbsp olive oil
2 tsp kosher salt
¼ cup [85 g] maple syrup

1 Preheat the oven to 400°F [200°C] with a rack positioned in the center. Line a rimmed baking sheet with nonstick aluminum foil or regular foil sprayed with nonstick spray.

2 Cut the squashes in half crosswise. Remove the seeds and pulp. Place the squashes cut-side down on a cutting board and cut in half again. Cut each quarter into 1 in [2.5 cm] crescent-shaped slices.

3 Place the slices of squash onto the prepared baking sheet. Drizzle with the olive oil and season with the salt. Spoon the maple syrup onto each piece; flip over and coat the other side as well.

4 Roast the squashes in the oven for 15 minutes, flip the pieces over, and bake for an additional 15 minutes, until they're golden and starting to caramelize on the edges. Serve warm.

FOOD

Acknowledgments

WRITING A BOOK WAS NOT AN EASY FEAT for me. But luckily, I have some pretty amazing people in my life who have guided me through the process and given me the unconditional love and support to keep at it and achieve my dreams. Thank you to everyone who has allowed me to share my passion for autum in this lifestyle guide.

To my mom—thank you for always believing in me and encouraging me to major in something creative, even though I went to college right as the 2008 economic crisis hit. I'm truly blessed to have you as my biggest cheerleader. I wouldn't be half as successful without you in my life.

To Tom—the professional food and hospitality photographer in my life. Thank you for showing me that I can thrive as a creative and make my dreams into a reality. Also, thank you for shooting this book and for listening to all of my highs and lows with this crazy career as a content creator.

To my management team—Tami and Ben. Thank you for taking a chance on me, and for being so understanding when my mental health has been in the gutter. I truly wouldn't be where I am without you, and every day, I thank God that you're in my life.

To Rachel Stinson Vrooman and the Inn at Stinson Vineyards—thank you for letting me shoot a good chunk of the book at your gorgeous property. I will never get over those Blue Ridge Mountain views, and it was an honor to be able to photograph these recipes in my beautiful home state.

To Serena & Lily—thank you for loaning some gorgeous props for this shoot. Thank you to Fiori Floral Studio for providing flowers. And big thank you to Diana Jeffra and Lauren Healy for their incredible work with food and prop styling. I could not have made this happen without you!

And last, but certainly not least: Thank you to Claire and the team at Chronicle Books for taking a chance on me and helping me turn my passion into a book. I am forever thankful for your partnership and willingness to help this girl from Virginia share her love of the fall season with the world.

ALICIA TENISE CHEW is a lifestyle blogger and former East Coaster now based in LA. On her blog, *Alicia Tenise*, she writes about entertaining, fashion, beauty, food and drink, and travel. She has been featured in *ELLE Magazine*, *Essence*, the *Washington Post*, and *Washingtonian Magazine*, among others.

TOM MCGOVERN is a food and lifestyle photographer based in LA.